EVERYONE DESERVES TO SPARKLE

Vome Aghoghovbia

Copyright © 2016 Miss Vome Aghoghovbia

All rights reserved.

ISBN: **978-1539604921**

Library of Congress Control Number: **2016917502**

LCCN Imprint Name: **Charleston, SC**

This book is dedicated to my Abba, my Father.

Contents

INTRODUCTION

EVERYONE DESERVES TO SPARKLE

Everything has beauty, but not everyone sees it.

— Confucius

Are we meant to just live life day by day, moment by moment, as the wind blows? Is there a purpose for our days and seasons?

When I started understanding my uniqueness and realising that I deserve to sparkle, I started viewing life in a different way. Suddenly, life was not just about going to school, getting good grades, getting a great job, getting married, and being a nice person. These things are amazing and are fantastic aims, but it dawned on me that in addition, I am uniquely designed to do something special and specific. There is only one of me; there is something unique I can offer in a way that no one else can. I am here to use my unique design to make a difference that creates ripples.

From that moment, I felt like a light bulb lit in my head. Everything seemed brighter, as if colours had changed from saffron yellow to a bright, sun-streaked orange. It was a defining moment for me. I had grasped the importance of walking in the plan and purpose for my life, and I realised that each phase in my life is a stepping stone, a preparation for the next phase. The importance of navigating each season with diligence and persistence, even through storms, became clearer to me. I instantly understood it!

This new buzz led to a deeper desire for growth and more courage to stretch myself, to ask more questions and gain understanding. There was a hunger to continue finding and working on being all I am designed to be. From that moment, I was no longer the same. That is how purposeful living lightens us up.

Why do many of us live like we are only here to run through the daily routines of life? Why are we living like we are clones, when in fact we are so unique, made with such meticulous detail and extraordinary care that science tells us that out of about seven billion people in the world, our fingerprints belong to only us? Understanding my uniqueness changed the way I saw many things. The way I thought was transformed, the way I saw life evolved, and the way I saw myself changed, too. I deserve to *sparkle*…and so do you!

Uniqueness cannot be put into a bubble. It does not mean you have to be witty or brainy or eccentric or stand out with vivid colours.

Uniqueness does not mean trying to be different or doing something different. You just have to be you. Understanding, enhancing, and utilising—*discover, appreciate, develop and use your gifts, abilities, passions, experiences*—what you have to offer to make a difference.

I was born into a generation known as the "millennials." Born between 1980 and 1995, we reached adulthood in an ever-changing time and have been privileged to witness the rapid evolution of technology. We were born at the advent of the Walkman, during the invention of Windows, and just at the brink of the conception of Google.

As a little girl, I was not a child you would have spotted and thought would go on to have a passionate love affair with mathematics and attain a first-class engineering degree. I had no interests in mathematics or science and was not great at them, either. School was really just a part of my daily routine, like brushing my teeth or eating breakfast.

Playing was ingrained in me as my favourite pastime. I was the little girl who would walk into a room, strike up a conversation with the next person and make five new best friends in the same breath. I was animated and fun-loving. My interests were singing and dancing for hours to Disney songs and spending days writing songs and raps for a girl band I formed with my childhood friends, Onyeka and Omono.

The highlight of my day was waking up at sunrise to watch the Cartoon Network channel and playing an adventure shark-and-fire game I created with my immediate older sister, Vese.

Storytelling was my deep passion. I would often spin up unending tales about the lion and the tortoise being "frenemies," and then compel my sisters, Voke, Vona, and Vese to sit and listen to my stories until their ears hurt.

I loved going to Ikoyi Club, a country club in the upmarket area of Ikoyi in Lagos, Nigeria. Still learning how to swim, I would waddle and paddle until my eyes were red and sometimes until the lifeguard said it was time for under twelves to leave the swimming pool due to club rules. Growing up, I was encouraged to thrive, embrace my creativity and stretch myself. Somewhere along the way, through different occurrences, I discovered other gifts and talents hidden within.

If someone had asked me then if I would one day work for Google and have a passion for solving complex problems, I might have laughed, because as a child, that was not who I was.

Years later, I look back and realise that the bouncy little girl with the ponytails was instrumental in shaping me into who I am today.

Now, as a young woman who has, through the years, experienced diverse cultures, education in great institutions, rapid technological advancement, and diverse work experience in different companies like BP, Deloitte, and Google, one of my struggles has been discovering and understanding my uniqueness in this ever-changing, busy world of diverse views and experiences.

The process of evolving through self-discovery, diverse experiences and observing life's seasons made me realise that beauty truly is in the journey. I have come to realise that I deserve to sparkle in this ever-buzzing world around me, and the process of evolving is a key ingredient to the realisation of that sparkle.

Many people have a desire to understand who they are. They want to understand their uniqueness, know what they have been designed to do and what they have to offer. Most importantly, they want to know how to achieve this purpose.

With all the perks that come with the world we live in today, we also live in a world shaped by instant gratification that does not value process. Our continuous connectedness through social media and technology means we get communication, information, and entertainment in real time, on demand.

We can read the history of a country with the touch of a button on a Google search page, instantly upload videos to YouTube and download music in seconds straight to our devices. When I shop online, one of the first things I look for is options for free or next-day delivery. Amazon, the online-retail giant, brought happiness my way when it started same-day delivery services.

Speaking with friends I have not seen in years, I feel like no time has passed due to ease of communication and regular social-media updates. With the Uber app, I no longer need to store cab companies' phone numbers. I can get a ride within seconds, with payments taken directly from my account.

As an engineer and a technology enthusiast, I value technological advancement and the ease it brings to our world;

however, as technology evolves at a rapid pace, I find that our patience grows thinner while our need for instant gratification increases. Sometimes we forget that some things take time.

There is a process to discovering and understanding our unique design. There is beauty in the process of finding the purpose for our unique design and developing ourselves to fit that purpose. Within that process lies a sparkling journey that should be enjoyed and embraced.

I truly began to sparkle the moment I started understanding who I was specially designed to be. I started to truly blossom when I grasped that I was in a beautiful process of fully becoming that person. This book was birthed from my ongoing process and a burning desire to see others embrace themselves and know that they deserve to sparkle!

Remember, you are a star! Keep shining.

CHAPTER 1

THE EVOLVING BUTTERFLY

*We delight in the beauty of the butterfly but rarely admit the changes
it has gone through to achieve that beauty.*

— Maya Angelou

As a child, I was what you might call an explorer, with
a very active and curious mind. I would run around
my house for hours exploring, seeking and creating. For me,
learning facts at school always went beyond the four walls of
my classroom.

When I turned six, I learnt in science class that trees and
plants could grow from a tiny seed buried in the soil. I was intrigued and tried to wrap my head around how a minute seed,
smaller than my thumb, could transform into a huge tree. Having the knowledge alone was not going to cut it for me. I came
home, told my friends about this intriguing thing I learnt at
school and suggested we try it out.

Wanting to understand the how, why, and when, my friends

and I set out on a fact-finding mission. We got some sand, poured it into a bucket, shoved bean seeds in the sand, and poured a ridiculous amount of water into the bucket.

We waited for a week, taking turns peeking into the bucket, puzzled as to why our plant refused to grow. With downcast faces, we wondered what went wrong. We followed instructions by carefully putting the bucket under sunlight and thought, *The teacher said seed, soil, water, and sunlight was the winning combination, what happened?*

Disappointed by the lack of progress, and with a curiosity to solve the puzzle, I asked an older friend what else we needed to germinate the seed, as I vaguely remembered the teacher saying something about different types of soil. Then I was told about manure—cow dung. We wandered around, trying to think of where we could find this mysterious manure. After walking around for a while and not finding any cow dung, my active mind came up with an outlandish idea that was an interesting substitute for our cow-dung dilemma…

Our plant never grew, but I later came to understand that the knowledge I learnt at school was not wrong; it was my application of what I was taught that was deficient. I discovered that a great tree could really come out of a tiny seed buried inside the soil.

That day I learnt a very good lesson. If you decide to explore and take things further, your main plan may not work, but you are bound to discover or learn something new along the way. This lesson encouraged me to never stop thinking and analysing how things work.

Of all the things that intrigued me, butterflies were one of the most captivating. It was complex to understand, as a little child, how the creeping caterpillar, which looked like a millipede in my very young mind, could transform into such a stunning insect with dazzling wings.

There were just so many questions that were justified and reinforced by my curiosity. Where did the wings come from? How did the wings become so colourful? Is the caterpillar not saddened by its reality? Is it disappointed that it is not as vivid and nimble as the butterfly?

I could never understand why the insect had to become a caterpillar before transforming into a butterfly. It was a concept I never fully understood and did not stop trying to analyse.

Many people are drawn to the butterfly. My cute three-year-old niece, who is an absolute delight, loves butterflies. She crosses her delicate hands, flaps them like wings and, with a contagious giggle, screams, "Butterfly!" I can understand her fascination. Butterflies are beautiful, graceful insects with vivid, symmetrical wings; however, this attractive, marvellous creature did not just come to exist. It went through what I call a becoming transformation that was purposeful and necessary to bring about the masterpiece that it is.

No one says "as beautiful as the caterpillar." The caterpillar is not as celebrated as the butterfly; however, even though it is not immediately obvious, the caterpillar is a masterpiece in its own right with its unique purpose.

It is well known that before the stunning insect dazzles us and flaps its lovely wings, it starts out as an egg and transforms through four distinctive stages. Each stage fulfils a different purpose. The insect strives to get closer to its goal with each transformation, while every stage adds value towards the fulfilment of becoming a butterfly.

The beauty in realising that life is a process and that we are all meant to be in a process of growth and development, with an ideal purpose at every stage, is that we can begin to accept ourselves. We can accept all we were previously and all we are now whilst striving to be better.

The way we have been designed is not accidental. Every inch of who we are to the last detail—our *form, gifts, talents*—is not by chance.

Take off your shoes and look down at your toes. You may or may not like the way they look, but even the little things we pay no attention to, like the shape and length of our toes, are not accidental. There are many distinctive functions we have been designed for.

There are seven key factors to understanding our unique design and using that unique design to make a difference. The chapters in this book explore navigating *seasons*, understanding *process*, birthing *newness*, experiencing *growth*, undergoing *transformation*, enjoying *fruition* and making *impact*. These factors contribute to our sparkle. Throughout the chapters, there are activities called "Work out/Engage" which will help you further engage with the book.

Remember, you are unique! Keep striving to be your best self.

CHAPTER 2

SEASONS: THE PERIODIC BEAUTY

The sun shines different ways in winter and summer. We shine different ways in the seasons of our lives.

— Terri Guillemets

Somewhere along the line, the adventurous child who loved the outdoors grew up to become a homebody. As time went on, I began to relish the simple pleasures of being indoors.

Being a homebody means winter is a great excuse to do the things you love. For me it is spending time with family, staying cosy and wrapped up indoors, bingeing on Netflix or reading a good book and drinking my special DVees hot chocolate with marshmallows melting into whipped and ice cream.

The summer comes, the weather changes, and I try not to stay completely in my own bubble. There is a lot more activity during the summer, which means doing other things I love as well, such as basking in the sun, dancing in a bright summer dress, and having barbeques in gardens. Other times, I find myself going outside my comfort zone like taking a random trip to Hyde Park to hire and relax in a pedal boat. Do you not love the ever-changing seasons and the changes they bring?

Life happens in seasons. Ideal seasons come with optimal conditions to aid a specific activity. Each of the four seasons comes at defined times, and each has a different condition and purpose.

Our preferences tend to change based on the season. For instance, many prefer ice cream and frozen treats during the summer, but when winter comes along, their taste buds crave hot chocolate and steaming hot cuppas.

In some cases, our preferences do not change, but we are forced to move with the times and seasons. No matter how much we adore or loathe our winter coats, gloves, and woolly scarves, when winter arrives, we fish out warm clothing. Once it's summer, our warm clothing stays in our wardrobe and storage boxes, and out come the summer shorts, T-shirts, and maxi dresses.

Every season has its allure and character. Many prefer summer to winter, but there is a delicate exquisiteness to winter that cannot be fully harnessed in the summer. There is also a delight in the summer that cannot be fully appreciated in the winter.

Winter is picturesque in nature—the way snow delicately falls in little flakes from the sky and sits on trees, cars, and rooftops in a whiteness that dazzles. In the summer, heatwaves and insects buzzing in ears might be pests, but during this season, the skies are crystal blue, the sun a bright orb in the sky and flowers a burst of colours as they come to bloom. It is in this season that outdoor activity thrives, as something about the warmth fuels people with a desire to explore and engage in activities.

Spring and autumn have their allure; there is an autumn timelessness that spring cannot supply, and an "easy, breezy" feeling and sense of renewal spring brings that autumn is unable to provide.

Spring brings with it sudden light showers, but April showers bring bursting buds and blossoming trees, which are an instant attraction to sun-seeking butterflies. As summer gives way to autumn, leaves begin to fall; a scenic array of red, brown, orange and yellow leaves fall in lakes, on the streets, on benches and create a classic scenery like something out of a painter's canvas.

The four seasons are distinctly different, but each shines in its own special way. Different seasons in our lives have their own allure and character, and each comes with a unique purpose and challenge. We shine in different ways in the seasons of our lives. How can we embrace, navigate and thrive in the different seasons that life brings?

The Four Seasons

Plan for the season. I have this habit: I find the idea of carrying umbrellas around to be cumbersome. During spring, even though I know it is bound to rain, I step out of the house without an umbrella! This is because a part of me is thinking, *It might not rain today*. It is a gamble I almost always regret taking because when the clouds start to darken, and the sky rumbles as it signals the arrival of rain, I start to wish I had taken my umbrella out with me. Some other days, I can see the problem about to unravel and I still take the risk. I see that the clouds are heavy, and it looks like it might rain, but I take the risk and go out without my umbrella. I think to myself, *Who wants to carry an umbrella around all day. It might only drizzle*. I find it amusing that it is on days like this when I refuse to plan for the weather that it tends to rain the most. Even though I am aware of the possibility of an event happening—in this case, rain—I am often caught out in the consequences because I am not prepared! There are times when it is obvious that a situation is developing while other times you only get a subtle hint; however, in both cases failure to

Work out/Engage

What season are you in? Consider this in different areas of life. As an example, using "career" answer questions like: What career am I in? What level am I at? What season does my level identify with? How do I feel about the season?

Illustration/Aid

A sixty-year-old has spent thirty years in insurance and is about to retire. This would be your autumn season; you might be at a stage where you are ready to wind down, following an accomplished career. You may also want to make changes to suit your new life.

plan has repercussions.

We are in certain seasons in different areas of our lives; discerning that season will help us understand how we need to respond. If we see that the skies are grey and understand the effect of the rain, we should prepare and take an umbrella in anticipation.

Let me give an example of a young man's career to illustrate my point. This young man, who started his career a couple of years back as an analyst at an accounting firm, is in a spring season, which involves "budding." I like to term it as the beginning, the time with aspirations and hope for the future. Compare this to a director who is twelve or fifteen years into her career and is aiming for chief operating officer (COO). Her career would be in what I would call the summer season, a period that is characterised by activity and results. Understanding time and seasons teaches us how we need to respond and move optimally with the season.

Seasons help us focus. When a butterfly is in the chrysalis, it focuses on its transformation and does not attempt to fly from flower to flower like a butterfly. In that chrysalis stage, it is not equipped to fly, as it does not have fully developed wings. Understanding seasons helps us focus and prioritise what is most important to do within that time frame.

"*There is a season for everything and a time for every delight and event or purpose.*"[1] Although we can do various things at different times, there are certain activities that yield the best results with

---

1   Ecclesiastes 3:1 (Amplified Bible).

the conditions of a particular season. For instance, it is possible to learn to speak a new language at sixty, but it is a lot easier to do at six. At six, the brain is still developing and absorbs things much quicker, making this an ideal season to learn a new language.

Let's go back to the example of the young man who is in the spring (budding) season of his career. This phase requires exploration and building a strong foundation by learning and growing exponentially. Starting out a new career brings about a fresh slate to start writing a new story.

Understanding this means he can capitalise on the season by asking many questions, increasing knowledge and learning many skills. It is the best time to try out diverse things, to have wide-ranging experiences and to realign and change his career path if needed. This might be a good time to start out and make a good initial impression when he finally settles into his desired career. The season is not without challenges. Starting sometimes means a steep, fast-paced learning curve; however, understanding that "when it rains, it pours" will help you take an umbrella in anticipation. Be prepared to stumble a few times and stand up stronger, to overcome obstacles and maybe find someone more experienced in your chosen field who can show you the ropes.

Compare this to the compliance director who aims to be COO one day and is in a summer season. Though she is still learning and growing, the time with the steepest learning curve has passed. Now it is the time to produce plenty results. She would have produced great results while training in her spring season; however, she is at a place where she can produce more results with firmer feet.

Understanding this means she can capitalise on the season by churning out continuous high-quality production. This season is not without challenges, either. As time progresses and the learning curve begins to plateau, there is a risk of complacency, of no longer seeking opportunities to learn and grow. She might stop seeking new ways of doing things due to too much focus on production and neglecting other things.

Sometimes, the best way to overcome this is by mentoring someone who is in his or her spring season in that area of life.

> **Work out/Engage**
>
> *What is the purpose of the season you are in? Highlight three advantages and two challenges of this season. What can you do to capitalise on the advantages? What can you do to navigate the challenges?*

By showing others the ropes, sharing your challenges and how you overcame, you build them up, but you also remain relevant and learn new things from them.

Blossom and fail forward. Let us go back to my previous example about being unprepared for the rain. The chances are that, after being unexpectedly beaten by rain, your mood and day might have been affected and your clothes possibly ruined, but it is almost certain that you would learn from that experience and hopefully plan better next time. Seasons are ever changing; we cannot stop them from happening, but we can plan properly in order to thrive in the new season. Sometimes we are in blooming times, and other times we are right in the storm. Learning to thrive in blooming times and withstanding the storms can help start a revolution!

Rowland Hussey Macy was the American businessman who is famous for starting the department store company called Macy's. Starting from small, humble beginnings, he transformed the store into a massive retail chain that is still well-known and thriving till this day.

He had several failed businesses before he started Macy's. At the age of thirty-six, after many futile retail ventures, his past experiences, perseverance, determination and creativity worked in his favour as he set up Macy & Co.

At the age of fifteen, he worked on a whaling ship, but he soon realised the pay was not a good enough reward for the work he was putting in. He decided to look for other opportunities available to him, and, inspired by Benjamin Franklin's accomplishments, he started a printing apprenticeship at the age of nineteen. Soon after, he discovered printing was not the right fit for him and he decided to move on to seek other opportunities.[2]

Macy went on to open his first dry-goods store, and over the next ten years, he was unsuccessful at four retail ventures. Despite his failures in his business attempts, these early circumstances of trying, failing, learning, growing and bouncing back were incredibly valuable later in his life for his future business, a blessing in disguise. On this journey towards achieving his goal

---

2   Keri Hanson, "The History of Macy's: From Humble Beginnings to Stunning Success," Visit Macys, last modified June 9, 2015, http://www.visitmacysusa.com/blog/history-macys-humble-beginnings-stunning-success.

for the store, he might have been called a perpetual failure by people who, short-sightedly, could not see beyond his current state. They might have failed to see that Macy was a hardworking man who was determined to not let his challenges deter him.

In 1851, he opened the Haverhill store, which failed; but thirty-six-year-old Macy made a strong comeback. He bounced back as he moved to New York City and finally opened R. H. Macy & Co in 1858.[3]

Being the man he was, he applied what he had learnt from his past experiences to come up with trailblazing and leading-edge initiatives for retail management. Macy started innovative business practices; he offered fixed prices for the same item rather than giving opportunities for the standard bargaining, and he offered lower prices for cash acquisitions in a time most shoppers bargained and used credit. As his business expanded and he was offered credit, he refused and stuck to his principles of working solely with cash.

Despite a recession, Macy's business grew. He was operating in a different economy, as those were booming years for the store. The business became a forerunner known for innovation as he developed unique marketing strategies that established and set precedence for the retail industry as we know it today. Macy learnt from different stages in his life and ended up becoming a man known for many firsts that changed the face of retail.

Every time we take children to see Santa in stores, we

3   Ibid.

should thank Rowland Hussey Macy for being first to feature an in-store Santa Claus during the holidays. He had some other innovative ideas such as having themed store exhibitions and lighted window displays to attract customers, giving rise to the concept of "window shopping."[4]

Macy is also known for more inspiring firsts as he made history by being the first retailer to promote a woman, Margaret Getchell, to an executive position. She helped build Macy's to the innovative and thriving retail department store it is today.

Being an innovator, Macy saw that his store was away from the main shopping area and realised he had to come up with creative ways to attract customers. Knowing how to put past experience to good use, he used his printing industry experience to start distinctive newspaper advertising campaigns that were mostly unseen by any of his competitors.

Macy understood seasons; he knew how to learn from stormy seasons and position himself to thrive in blooming times. This helped him move from small beginnings to running a massive, thriving retail store.

Work out/Engage

Are you in a new academic or financial year? Or perhaps a new phase? Consider the previous year or phase. Highlight three things you accomplished, areas you developed and things you were commended for. Highlight two areas you fell short and things you could have done better or achieved.

Reflecting on areas of failings can be a learning activity to prevent reoccurrence, learn lessons and understand ourselves better. This helps us fail forward as we can use those learning points to prevent us from making the same mistakes. It might seem obvious that we should learn from past mistakes; but like with my rain and umbrella situation, many of us do not apply our learning. It is making that conscious effort to apply the lessons learnt that makes all the difference.

When we get into the habit of considering areas where we fall short and understanding what led to it, as well as highlighting areas where we need to grow, we attain a deeper level of self-awareness and understanding. This can help us discover our Achilles heels.

Learn from the past and plan for the future. Phases from our past gives us unique insight that can be used to steer the next phase.

As one chapter in our life ends and we are about to step into the next, it is good practice to reflect on the previous chapter. This could be reflecting on the past year as we step into a new year or reviewing our performance in our past jobs when we are starting new roles. Even as we move to a different phase in life, be it transitioning from being a student to starting work in a paid job, or even from being single to getting married and eventually becoming a parent, with each move from one phase to the other, it helps to reflect on the past phase.

There is a story of a jolly man who drove a red cab in a small town. He was the town's most loved cab driver. Although he was not the best driver, and his cab was not the nicest, it was always a unique experience to ride in his car.

From the time he picked up his passengers till he dropped

them off, he made them feel like they were the only ones in the world. He would remember all the things they shared with him on their last car ride and ask about progress with genuine interest. He would ask about their day with a warm smile and offer solutions to their many problems.

His passengers looked forward to going around in his cab. They anticipated the advice he gave and the unique insights he had to offer. He was different to other cab drivers because he was skilled at looking beyond ferrying his passengers around. He went deeper by understanding their uniqueness; however, the jolly man soon started to feel inadequate and sad. He felt he lacked skills to be a great driver.

Downcast, he left his house and went to sit in the town's local fish-and-chips shop. He looked through the window and gazed at the sky. One of his passengers came into the shop and, excited to see him, ran and sat next to him. "Joe, you are a star," the passenger said. "All your great ideas this year have helped me get great returns. You should be a coach!" Joe left the shop with a spring in his step and a dream in his heart to train as a coach.

Reflecting on the past is important as it teaches us a great deal about ourselves. It should be done to count our blessings, to analyse what has worked for us and areas we have grown. By reflecting, we are able to assess where we applied our greatest strengths, how we displayed our passions and what skills we developed in the process.

While the past is filled with previous achievements and lessons, the future is full of promise. It is crucial that we think about our future. A mental picture of what we want to be in five, ten, twenty, even fifty years lightens us.

Vision fuels motivation; having a vision of what we strive to be and what we aspire to achieve in life is a powerful tool. When times are challenging and obstacles come along the way, holding onto that mental picture can help us push through.

> **Work out/Engage**
>
> *Write down a vision for your life and your long-, mid- and short-term goals in different areas of your life. What do you want to be and achieve in one, five and fifteen years? Consider your unique design, interests, gifts, talents, passions and experiences.*

A clear vision motivates us in the right direction. It helps us be specific and intentional. It is recommended to take a further step beyond only thinking about future aspirations by also writing them down. This gives life to the dreams in our head and provides an opportunity to assess if what we hope for is actually right for us.

Bottom Line of the Periodic Beauty

Adapting requires patience and determination. There is a lot to learn from Rowland Macy. He learnt along the way and handled different seasons with perseverance and determination. He dared to dream, made a distinct impact and influenced the retail industry for many years.

Bring beauty out of unpleasant seasons. One of the most wonderful things about Macy's story is how he learnt effectively from his unsuccessful ventures and channelled them into making his future better. The fact that we fail does not make us failures; however, how we handle failure makes all the difference. Macy's story shows beauty can come from anything, but this might not be immediately clear to everyone.

Build character. Stormy seasons come to test us and build our character to enable us shine effectively in blooming times. Character is a major ingredient in our sparkle. When everything is said and done, what we stand for lasts. In this long zigzag journey of continuous development towards achieving our purpose, integrity will help us stand. Often times, we focus on smoothening our covering—*looks, skills, abilities*—without also focusing on our character.

There is brilliance in your unique experiences, *your achievements, successes and opportunities*. Beauty can also come out of ashes, out of *challenges, struggles* and even *failures*. There is value in knowing what season you are in, in understanding the season, and in preparing for how to navigate the season. You are wonderful at every stage as you strive to grow and develop to further discover your unique attributes and make a difference.

Remember, you are in a season! Keep embracing and navigating it.

CHAPTER 3

PROCESS: THE UNRAVELLING GRACE

If you are walking down the right path and you are willing to keep walking, eventually you will make progress.

— Barack Obama

A few months ago, my siblings and I ordered Singaporean fried rice and spicy salt and chilli chicken wings from an online food delivery service. As proud lovers of food, or foodies as we like to call ourselves, we waited in anticipation for our food, and it felt like an unbearable, weeklong wait. As seconds trickled into minutes, we began to glance at the clock with anticipation fused with an increasing dissatisfaction. After painfully waiting for an hour, the food arrived. I laughed as it dawned on me that waiting is becoming a fading concept.

In a time when many people will be frustrated with standard delivery services, immediacy is becoming the expectation. Instant delivery is becoming the norm thanks to online retail giants like ASOS and Amazon. People want to be able to order all kinds of things and have them immediately available.

It is said that millennials prefer experiences to things. For instance, some prefer to spend more on a wedding or honeymoon than an actual engagement ring; however, one thing that crosses across all generations is the love for diamonds. While we may be able to walk into a jewellery store and acquire diamonds with the swipe of a card, the reality is that the diamond has a story that does not involve immediacy.

Each diamond goes through a process that unravels its grace. It goes through a rigorous process from when it is formed in the ground through to when it is put on the market. This process involves extreme temperature and pressure, mining, sorting, cutting and polishing to perfection. It is this process that lead to the dazzling gem displayed in a jewellery store.

Process brings out our unique sparkle to the greatest extent possible, but this takes time. How can we evolve through a process to bring out our unique sparkle to a greater degree?

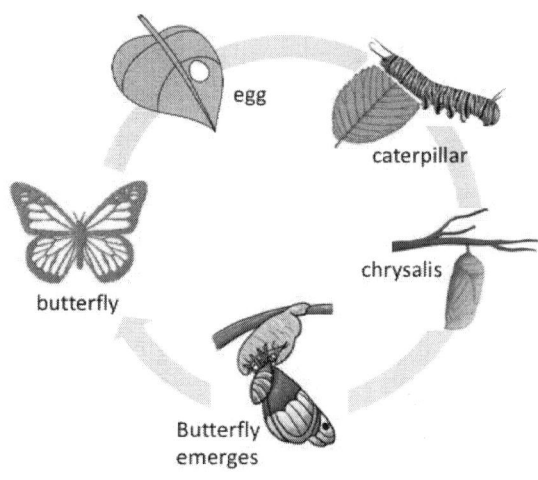

The Butterfly Lifecycle

The butterfly process. I have seen myself go from egg to caterpillar to chrysalis and then blossom into a butterfly in different areas of my life. There are also areas where I have not progressed as quickly as expected, and I find that I remain creeping in the caterpillar stage for a while. It is interesting to note that there are other areas of my life where I have not started this process due to various factors like seasons and prioritisation. That said, I am excited by the endless possibilities that lay ahead, knowing that the few processes I have undergone have impacted my life tremendously.

One area where I am still evolving is around my tendency to be shy. I went from being a child who was confident and animated to a preteen who became extremely shy. As an imaginative and expressive seven-year-old, I spent my time writing numerous songs, creating choreographies for the songs and boldly performing them with my girl band. I could not sing to save my life, but we would rehearse the songs and perform them on Friday evenings during our weekly fellowship.

At that age, I also discovered I loved to write poems, fiction and nonfiction. I would write several poems, taking the time to ensure that the words rhymed. After learning about different types of poems at school, I started trying to write sonnets, as I guessed a ballad was a bit of a stretch for me.

One of my favourite stories was "Goldilocks and the Three Bears." I progressed from telling it to creating and narrating my own version of the classic to anyone who would listen at home. My immediate older sister would laugh that my stories were never ending, and even though she had other things to do, she always found the time to listen to me as my very young mind tried to put characters and scenes together.

At the time, I had not become a book worm. I was doing decently at school. My participation in extracurricular activities was high, and I was not timid in applying myself to school activities. In some ways, I was reserved. I was never the first child to raise her hand up in class, but if I was ever called upon, I would perform with no reservations.

At school, I played basketball and read the daily news during assembly. I took part in debates and numerous dances and recited a poem for the graduation ceremony. I even tried out drumming, but I was terrible at it!

I was not the best at everything I attempted, but I was willing to try and give things my best shot. When I think of my younger self, I often applaud how brave I was.

By the age of twelve, I had become extremely shy. The change was a result of a combination of two things. The first stemmed from the fact that I was the only child at home at that time, which somehow made me retrieve into a shell. Prior to that, I always had my sisters around. We always did things together: playing, planning meals, learning new songs and dances. Once they left Nigeria to study in England, I began to live like an only child. This lasted for six years, with the exceptions being the holidays when we were all together.

In addition, I became an adolescent who started becoming more aware of my surroundings and trying to understand myself. I am not sure which had more of an impact, but the combination resulted in me becoming extremely shy and being in my own world most of the time. I loved the being-in-my-own-world part, but shyness came with its limitations. I found that crippling shyness was less than ideal; it can limit you from great opportunities and suppress your abilities.

In my case, shyness stole my desire to express my creativity and my readiness to participate in extracurricular activities, and it restricted me from doing anything that put focus on me.

As my participation in extracurricular activities plummeted, my academic performance rose, especially in mathematics and science. As a happy geek, I developed an unashamed love for mathematics. It grew so strong that till this day, when I am bored, I solve many mathematical problems just for fun.

In secondary school, I usually came out with top results in mathematics, further mathematics and biology. I also did exceptionally well in physics, English literature and economics, while languages were my weakest subjects.

With each year that passed in secondary school, I fell more in love with learning and performed better. As I was building momentum academically, I was also at a place where I would rather not attempt anything I did not have to. I avoided being involved in activities, especially any that involved me being in the spotlight.

The problem was, I was getting comfortable with not stretching myself or stepping out of my comfort zone. This continued until I came to a stage of realisation, which is usually the first step towards fruition.

The day of realisation came when one of my aunts came to stay with us for a few weeks. Prior to that, the last time she visited was when I was ten years old. During that visit, we had spent hours talking together, and as usual, I told her a few of my short stories. She told my mum she had enjoyed my company and was impressed by my seemingly effortless ability to interact with and speak to adults comfortably and respectfully. This impression led to her giving me a nickname, *Amaye*, which means "small woman." She reckoned that even though I was ten years old, I looked like a six-year-old who spoke like a grown woman!

The next time she came over, I was fourteen. She noticed that I hardly spoke more than a few words and could not hide her surprise at the change. She remarked that I was no longer speaking and conversing with the same assuredness I had back then. I had become a teenager who only spoke around people I was extremely comfortable with.

Hearing my aunt highlight the drastic change was a light-bulb moment for me! I realised I needed to get over this crippling shyness. I needed to learn to stop restricting what was in me. I realised I somehow picked up this bashful shyness along the way, and if I could learn to be *crippled* by shyness, I could learn to be *uncrippled* by shyness.

The dream was to be myself whilst trying my best to not be limited from being all I was created to be and do. The aim was to reduce the effects of this limiting shyness and start daring to act again. The process started, and it is probably one of the things I have worked on the most. Even though I came to a point of realisation at fourteen, it was not until years later that I started actively trying to break out of it.

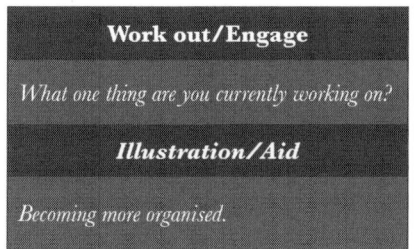

Work out/Engage

What one thing are you currently working on?

Illustration/Aid

Becoming more organised.

The problem is not with being shy; the point is that we should not be limited by anything from being all we have been created to be.

Know the worth of the transformation. Understanding the value of what we are working towards motivates us to go for it with tenacity. For me, it was realising that I was losing the ability to stretch myself and the boldness to get involved that the seven-year-old me had. Thus, I was wasting what was in me.

After the realisation, preparation and change in mind-set, I started the daily work of trying to grow. I went from being the person who gave a speech in my first year at university with my voice trembling, avoiding eye contact and dreading every moment of it, to addressing a crowd at a seminar with a degree of nervousness but actually enjoying it. I transformed from being at meetings, bursting with ideas but not saying one word to sharing *some* thoughts at small groups.

At different internships, managers said, "You are very intelligent and hardworking; try and speak at meetings so you do not hide your abilities." They said, "You have great ideas. Do not allow others take credit for your work and ideas." I started working to develop!

Being quiet and reserved are great; they were not the problem. The problem was I had been suppressing what was uniquely deposited in me for a while, and that was to no one's advantage. It was not benefitting the people around me; neither was it building me up.

In secondary school, the teachers were shocked that I delivered a manifesto that they described as powerful and inspiring when I was running for the post of assistant head girl. I had been in the school for years and had suppressed certain abilities. Even though I was quite involved in school, no one really knew I was capable of producing something so powerful.

The day I gave that speech, which eventually got me elected, I intentionally had to block out the thoughts that were screaming, "Do not attempt!" and had to strongly suppress all the shyness that was being triggered in my body.

I had to remind myself *(and I still constantly do)* that I am uniquely designed for a purpose that is beyond me. Suppressing what is in me is wasteful. We have all been gifted with unique abilities and talents to make an impact, and using those gifts makes an impact that goes beyond us.

As a firm believer in being yourself, I knew that the solution was not to change my personality with a predominant part of it being calm and reserved, but rather to continue to be myself while taking the time to grow in certain areas.

In my final year edition of my secondary-school magazine, I was described as "shy, reserved, unassuming Vome who can't hurt a fly [but] gave a powerful speech that won her the post of assistant head girl." I laughed at what I thought was a concise and exact description.

That description is probably still accurate; however, in addition to that, the shy part has evolved as I am learning to not be limited by that side of me.

I am learning to develop and smooth the aspects of my life that need smoothing. This involves learning to not limit myself by attempting to do new things, daring to act and learning to not be deterred from opportunities that will enable me thrive fully. At the point of realisation, I discovered there is much more to me: some I knew, some I

Work out/Engage

Highlight one thing that has been holding you back from using your gifts and highlight three ways to stretch yourself.

was in the process of discovering and some waiting to be discovered.

Stretching can be uncomfortable. Trying to go against the grain or stretching beyond your comfort zone is not a fairy tale; it will not always be beautiful roses, rainbows and sunshine. There were times I was frustrated and could not understand why I could not break out of this restrictive shyness when it was clearly holding me back. I thought, *I have the desire to break out of it, so why can I not do it instantly?*

My great, industrious, hardworking father has always encouraged my siblings and me to shoot for the stars. So I did just that. During my A-levels, I wrote a five-year plan, which had six things I wanted to achieve.

This was my five-year plan:

> » *Achieve at least A*AA at A-levels*
>
> » *Study chemical engineering at one of my three dream universities: University of Cambridge, University College London (UCL) or Imperial College.*
>
> » *Graduate with a first class degree*
>
> » *Do at least two major internships during my undergraduate degree*
>
> » *Work for ExxonMobil or L'Oreal, Apple or Google*
>
> » *Explore a potential interest in investment banking through an internship*

My wonderful father supported me through his encouraging words, which often felt like he was holding my hand over the phone throughout the whole university application process. He has such a deep desire to see his children succeed that he guided me throughout the process of selecting my A-level subjects to my degree to making university choices.

I remember clearly when I got the letter of invitation for my Cambridge interview. I was standing in my school corridor, expectantly holding the letter from Cambridge. I opened it and quickly called my family to tell them, "I got an interview!"

Although mathematics is my passion, I had also fallen in love with chemistry and physics; and so I felt prepared for the questions I would get at a chemical engineering interview.

I arrived at the beautiful Pembroke College at Cambridge University the night before my interview. The beauty and grandeur of the college met my expectations. It was the college of poets and scientists, thinkers and players, people who want to make a difference to the world. *Sounds like what I want to be*, I thought to myself as I watched the scene adoringly. I was not sure which of my three universities I wanted to go to, but the scene before me was convincing.

As I soaked in the environment, I started becoming nervous. I had heard so many horror stories from people and various websites about interviews that ended up in disaster.

I woke up the next morning; it was a bit chilly, and I felt uncertain in that vast college. I knew I should not be feeling wary, but nerves took over. I went into the interview room, sat down and, unable to make eye contact with the female interviewer, I began to answer her questions.

I could not survey my surroundings or take time to appreciate the interview room. I have no recollection of how long I was there for because of how frozen I was. My heart began to pound. I was too nervous to think clearly, and I began saying words to make the time pass. I froze!

I was asked to draw the graph for a formula, and I drew it diagonally. Immediately after I left the room, I thought, *Vome, what is wrong with you?* There was hardly any question I did not know the right answer to, or at least have an idea of what steps to take if I had taken my time, but I allowed nerves to cloud my thinking. As I walked back to my room in the lovely college, I knew the graph was obviously a straight, horizontal line. I knew that inside out, so why did I draw it diagonally? My nine-year-old self would have nailed this interview with confidence!

I did not get the Cambridge offer. I was slightly disappointed and frustrated with myself, more because I froze than anything else. I ended up achieving my desired grades and going to one of my dream universities, UCL, to study chemical engineering.

My experience at UCL taught me that beauty can come out of your struggles. You can still have that breathtaking moment of fruition at the end of the day. When I started at UCL, it became clear that was where I was supposed to be. It was part of the story. At UCL, I grew, transformed and got a clearer, more defined understanding of who I was.

There was something so amazing about walking in front of the UCL Main Quad building (a white stone building surrounded by grass and paths that lay just beyond the main gates). The first time I saw the Quad, I fell in love with the magnificent architecture. Its beauty surpassed my expectations.

I thought studying mathematics would have been my dream, but chemical engineering ended up being very dear to me, particularly in my fourth year when I did my research project. It was an amazing research topic, and I had an excellent supervisor.

By the time I gave my research project presentation, I realised I was really on the verge of becoming a chrysalis in the area of attempting boldly. Compared to the first presentation I ever gave at UCL, body trembling and speaking at the speed of light due to nerves, I could speak up boldly; and I delivered my presentation in a way I never could have four years before.

During my time at university, there were many beautiful moments and a few challenges. All sorts of challenges came along the way, from being unwell to circumstances that made me unable to revise or even attend some lectures.

I ended up graduating with first class honours, scoring one of the highest marks in my research project (*which involved a presentation—the public speaking I once dreaded*). I was speechless! The last of the six goals on my five-year plan list was ticked off! The dreams seventeen-year-old me had were completely brought to life!

This experience taught me a great deal about the process of evolving. When I got my result, I was overwhelmed, and fully understood that there is a plan and purpose for everyone.

Sometimes we just need to stretch ourselves.

I needed to go through the process and challenges to learn and discover myself. I started learning who I was more clearly and striving to get a clearer understanding of my unique design—my *gifts, talents, strengths, weaknesses, breaking points, personality*. I started learning to be confident and bold in the way I was designed to be. I had to learn to understand the source and purpose of my abilities before I had the boldness to express it.

I still identify with that extremely shy girl, but I can no longer completely recognise her, and that is growth. It is when I speak to people that I fully grasp the extent to which I have grown because when I tell them that I was restricted by shyness, I can see some struggling to understand what I mean. They could probably reconcile with my being quiet and shy from time to time, but crippling shyness? No.

I made a decision to strive to start using my thoughts, ideas, feelings, experiences and who I was designed to be to achieve what I was designed to achieve at every stage. I decided to not wait to be a striking butterfly in every area of my life before deciding to make a positive impact.

The aim is to be charitable even when we do not have much, to use our skills even when they might not be as sharpened, be helpful and to give of ourselves to others in time and value. It is also to attempt, to dare to perform and do our best in our own unique way whether it is in an area that we are still an egg, caterpillar, a chrysalis or operating as a butterfly.

In recent times, I have been rediscovering my creative

streak in different areas and have been developing the boldness to give talks and share my thoughts. I have tried to push myself beyond my comfort zone by attempting to do things that will make me grow even when I am afraid.

I am finding my passion deepening; exploring through travel and reading many books. I am learning what it means to lead, but most importantly knowing what it means to be accountable, which is one of the most important things about leadership. It really does start with me and managing myself.

Ultimately, I have grown to do many things in my own reserved, calm way, some of which would have been impossible a year or two ago. One of the best feelings in the world is coming to a realisation of who we are created to be and growing into that person. There is a purpose for our lives that requires us to be impactful.

Stretching does not feel natural. When you take an object and begin to stretch it beyond its normal form, there is often some resistance. It feels unnatural every time I have to extend myself, but I find that with time, it gets less uncomfortable. Stretching myself sometimes requires swinging to the other extreme when trying to find the perfect balance; however, with time, I have realised that the ideal balance will be found.

I am not there yet, it is an ongoing process, but progress has occurred. I see myself getting closer day by day, and that, for

---

Work out/Engage

Identify three challenges of stretching yourself in the area you want growth. How can you manage them? Create checkpoints to check your progress and growth.

me, is beautiful. As we progress towards our goal, we should see the beauty of where we are and the purpose of that stage on the way to where we are going.

Process can include pain. As immediacy is becoming the norm in today's world, one thing that teaches us patience is the job market and application process. I marvel when I hear stories of the "good old days" when people only had one interview to get graduate jobs, and my jaw drops when I hear a rare story of getting a job through only sending in a CV. The graduate job application process now requires three online tests: numerical, verbal and logical; one group exercise; two case studies, one presentation and two interviews…if you are lucky!

Many know what it is like to be unemployed for years, made redundant, make three hundred applications and get one hundred rejections. It can be a struggle, knowing you deserve to sparkle in a time when companies seem determined to freely dish out rejections and redundancies.

On the road to getting a job, despite having excellent experience, going to a globally acclaimed university or attaining top results, many still meet with much frustration, confusion and many predictable and standard rejection e-mails: "After careful consideration, we regret to inform you that you have been unsuccessful…"

In this job market, the importance of a penultimate year internship is often stressed. It arms you with experience and the improved chance of getting a graduate job the next year. The fortunate ones will get a graduate job the summer before final year even starts! In my penultimate year, after making almost fifty applications—*I still have my job application spreadsheet*—and after several assessment days, getting to the final stage and meeting rejections, I was tired. I was exhausted but kept going and persisting.

It was March. I needed to revise for exams starting the next month. This was three months before the end of the academic year, the stress of writing many cover letters was setting in and I still did not have an internship offer. It did not help that penultimate year was also the most difficult and tasking year for me academically.

Working at Google was one of the goals on my five-year plan list. I had heard so many brilliant things about Google, about the culture and how it could compare with paradise. It was a dream I had spoken about passionately but did not give much thought to the reality of it happening.

After many applications and almost losing hope, I got an e-mail from Google. I thought, *Am I awake? This is my dream experience!*

I had jumped the first hurdle, and I was being called for an interview. Now, I had to overcome the mountain of the four interviews coming up. I was expecting to get unsolvable interview questions, you know, one of those "which came first, the chicken or the egg?" type questions.

Initially, I felt a bit like a fish out of water. I heard less than 1 percent of people who apply to Google get the job. What gave me the right to think I could actually get in? I shut down doubt and decided to reverse my thinking from negative to positive. I figured out that the worst that could happen was a rejection. A rejection would have been disappointing, but I was not going to give up before I found out if I could actually get in.

I prepared more for this than I had for any other interview. During the interview, I was given some analytical "guesstimations," but I found the questions to be blissful. This was significantly due to preparation, favour and shutting the door to doubt.

After several interviews with Google, which were the best set of interviews I had that year, I got an offer. When they called to notify me, I felt a mixture of joy and surprise. I was so elated, I started to jump and dance in the carefree manner I reserve for my house. My surprise stemmed from the fact that *Google* said my interview was so great and that I was an exceptional candidate! They said, "You were so good that we had to find a place for you!"

After rejections from some firms, I finally got a dream offer, which ticked off the fifth item on my five-year plan list. There was one more goal to go!

I realised my job application phase was a process. Feedback from prior interviews like "You are very bright, speak up," or "Get your points across in group exercises" were cutting and polishing me to be fully prepared when Google e-mailed. I was geared up for those series of interviews.

I am grateful for the prior rejections and feedback because they were preparing me for a dream experience. My last day at

Google involved a meeting with one of my managers and being given a book with a note in it, which read "You have been a great intern for my team at Google." Google was an experience I will never forget! I keep my Google "noogler hat" safely till today.

During my final year, as time approached to apply for a graduate role, I prayed and put in my best effort. After a few applications and rejections, I got a graduate job.

The rejections were still painful. I cried my eyes out the day two amazing companies—after getting so far in their assessment process—rejected me on the same day. This time something was different, though. I understood that I was in a process of being cut and polished. It was either not the right opportunity for me, or I needed to take the feedback and prepare better for the next opportunity.

Everyone's path is different. We embark on different journeys, which have tailor-made processes. Our experiences will be unique, as no two people are wired exactly the same way; neither will they do exactly the same thing during the course of their lives.

The key is to understand "our" process as well as what unique purpose our process is shaping us for. No area of development is too small or insignificant if it leads us to have the impact we were created for. It does not have to be a large-scale event for it to be a worthwhile process.

The cycle never stops. We should keep growing and striving to be better versions of ourselves; constantly evolving by developing our character, learning new skills, having new experiences and making greater impact with each experience. Process can be painful, but it can bring out our sparkle and beauty to a greater degree!

Bottom Line of the Unravelling Grace

Undergo the process to discover purpose. There are inspiring stories like that of Colonel Sanders, who, after losing his father at the age of six, found himself in charge of feeding and taking care of his younger brothers and sisters. He had his first job at the age of ten and, from then on, went on to have numerous jobs. At the age of fifty, he made his special, secret chicken recipe. At sixty-two, he travelled from restaurant to restaurant, pitching his chicken recipe. Colonel Sanders cooked batches of chicken and travelled across the country to restaurants, striking deals that paid him a nickel for every chicken the restaurant sold.[5] The first restaurant that he landed was located out of Salt Lake City, Utah. It became the first Kentucky Fried Chicken (KFC). In one year, the restaurant tripled its sales due to 75 percent of their revenue coming from the Colonel's secret recipe chicken.[6] Although fast food is controversial, his story shows that regardless of circumstances like age, it is never too late to start a journey that leads to fruition. There is value in

---

5   "Colonel Harland Sanders," Biography.com, accessed January 6, 2016, http://www.biography.com/people/colonel-harland-sanders-12353545.

6   Ibid.

evolving through a process with ongoing hard work and dedication.

Undergo the process to aid self-discovery. There is something deposited in each of us that the world needs. Suppressing or not using our gifts and talents for impact is like a useful and wonderful gift placed inside a lovely wrapped gift box that is never opened. We know there is something valuable inside the gift box, but we are allowing limitations stop us from opening the gift box. Do not be a wasted gift! Pick up that box, open it, reach in and bring out that valuable, superb gift you suppressed and have hidden inside of you.

No matter how much we may have been ruffled up, there is something special we have to offer. A diamond in a pigsty is still a diamond, just a diamond that needs retrieving and restoration. A diamond that has been covered up with dust is still a diamond, just a diamond that needs dusting. Hide a diamond under a heap of leaves, and it is still a diamond, just a hidden diamond. Calling a diamond plastic does not stop it from being a diamond; it is just a diamond that needs to be established for what it is. Regardless of the covering, we have something special inside of us that is valuable no matter what.

Just like you might go through an old bag or wallet and find money you forgot was there, try to find gifts you never knew were in you. Try things out and find undiscovered talents. Be you, use your gifts and talents, let your passions drive you and have impact.

We can be ourselves, utilise our gifts and express ourselves in our own way. If you are naturally quiet or naturally more outgoing, you can express and utilise your gifts in your own special way. And even though there will be need for adjustment from time to time, the key is to not leave your talents unused. It is really about embracing you and using what is in you to make a difference.

Step by step, day by day. With each day, I find myself more willing to ask questions, explore and share my thoughts. I find myself operating beyond my comfort zone, and I really believe there is a purpose for my life…and for your life. There is a reason I went through, and I am still going through, this transformation in this area. A marvellous work begins in our lives, bit by bit, towards developing us for a purpose. Regarding this shyness evolution, I am not yet a butterfly. I would say I am a caterpillar who is quite content about where she is now and on the verge of becoming a chrysalis. There are times I am frightened when I dare to act and use what is in me. When this fear comes, I close my eyes and try to jump right in. I remind myself that I made a decision to not be a wasted gift and that I will be all I was designed to be.

Looking deeper than just the delicate appearance of the butterfly, and watching how the insect endures changes at every captivating stage, it is clear there is more to its design. If a butterfly that is nowhere as complex as a human being can go through such awe-inspiring processes and be so magnificent, how much more you?

Remember, you are inspirational! Keep pushing through.

CHAPTER 4

NEWNESS: THE GREAT CONCEPTION

From humble beginnings comes great things.

— Unknown

The Christmas morning routine was jumping out of bed and running at the speed of light to the Christmas tree. Until I turned ten, the night before Christmas was spent with an uncontainable excitement. I knew that Santa was going to come the next day, which automatically meant that beautifully wrapped presents would be lined side by side, under the Christmas tree.

After dinner on Christmas Eve, I would leave snacks for Santa, with the fervent hope that he had received my many letters. Some of my sisters went as far as sleeping under the Christmas tree because they wanted to see Santa. Only for them to wake up the next morning with the gifts nicely decorated around them.

Growing up in a large family, we had a fun-filled Christmas and New Year tradition. On New Year's Eve, after talking and dancing at home, we would gather in Church as a family to pray and dance into the new year. Once the clock strikes midnight, we would hug each other, scream "Happy New Year!" and drive home to set up and enjoy the stunning display of fireworks. The feasting and partying always continued from sunrise till the end of the day. That is my best childhood memory. New Year's Day was particularly special. There was always something electrifying about that day.

Hitting midnight on New Year's Day marks the start of celebrations, fireworks, confetti, feasting and special events. People are excited and filled with joy, and they welcome in the New Year with family and friends.

One of the most famous New Year's celebrations is the very memorable and long-term tradition of the New Year's Eve ball drop in Times Square. As the clock gets closer to midnight, expectation runs high, and excitement is in the air. People are focused on the shining lights and bustling energy of Times Square.

At 11:59 p.m., as a giant ball begins to drop from One Times Square, millions of people unite their voices to count down to the final seconds of the year. As the clock hits midnight, the crowd bursts out, celebrating the beginning of a new year and the prospects of a year filled with hopes, dreams and possibilities.

In another part of the earth, many people line the Thames waterfront and assemble in Trafalgar Square, London, waiting for the city to explode and be electrified in a dazzling display of vivid colours and sparks. At midnight, Big Ben's famous *bongs* ring out and the focus turns to the London Eye as the famous wheel produces a spectacular, swirling fireworks display.

Different countries welcome in the New Year in their own special way and with a unique flavour. One of the most beautiful New Year celebration displays is in Sydney, Australia. As people come to the waterfront to celebrate the New Year, the iconic Sydney Harbour Bridge ignites at midnight with one of the most spectacular fireworks productions.

The family-oriented New Year's celebrations in Nigeria are very exciting as many people dance into the New Year. As the clock hits midnight, they celebrate with family and loved ones as voices of well wishes ring out. Some go outside to set off fireworks in groups till the early hours of the morning. The rest of the day is filled with feasting, celebrations and giving food, gifts and well wishes to neighbours, friends and family.

There is something enthralling about new beginnings or starting again that gets people buzzing and excited. Many love New Year's Day because it represents progress or a fresh start. In anticipation, many start writing out New Year's resolution and make plans for the year.

The previous year is now in the past. What we failed to achieve on our goal list is now in the previous year. We count our blessings from the year before and look forward to the promise of the New Year.

The uncertainty that comes with new beginnings can be daunting, but when we welcome it with excitement, we begin to look forward to the endless possibilities.

I remember clearly the day my nephew was born. I had spent the night tossing and turning, and once it was morning, I dashed out of bed and headed to the hospital. The first time I set eyes on him and cradled him, I fell in love with him. It was a deep, instant love that I find hard to fully describe in words. It was as if he had always been part of my life.

There was a certain look in his eyes that captured my heart. It was the excitement, the twinkle in his eyes that felt as though he was ready to take on the world. I remember thinking, *This baby has a blank book, and he gets to write his story from today. He gets to start experiencing and growing. A completely fresh slate.* I was eager and excited for him at the endless possibilities and at the prospects of all he could be and all he could achieve.

Every day as he goes on to achieve many firsts—from the first time he started squirming, to when he mustered strength to crawl, to the moment he took his first step and walked, to the second he said a clear word. With each first, my heart melts all over again as he continues to fill in the pages of his book.

Newness is refreshing and enthralling. How can we embrace fresh starts, build a strong foundation and take the first step towards fruition?

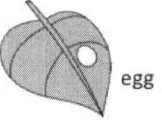

egg

Great conceptions are like butterfly eggs. Many great things start small. Butterflies start off as very minute eggs, like the size of a pinhead. In the same vein, many dreams start with a small, minute thought in the mind. This minute thought grows based on the surrounding conditions, how it is fed and the effort and care put into it.

Butterfly eggs have different hatching times and vary in colour and shape. They can be oval, round or cylinder-shaped. They also differ in texture; being smooth, rough or crumpled. Our dreams and ideas will come in different shapes, sizes, designs and nature. We all have different talents and levels of ability…almost like butterfly eggs.

Some female butterflies lay many eggs, but only few of the eggs make it to adulthood. Although we have many dreams, few are birthed. Many of us have big dreams. We have plans to improve ourselves backed with visions and the hope of fulfilment, but many do not get to see their dreams materialise.

We see that butterflies lay their eggs in suitable conditions; they are laid somewhere safe, sheltered from the elements of the harsh weather conditions, and the eggs are supported and protected. In the same vein, dreams need the right conditions to hatch.

When we have dreams, we need the right environment and tools to turn the thoughts in our heads into active goals that will survive. There needs to be suitable conditions to take our vision, ideas, and development aspirations from minute thoughts to reality. We need the ideal preparation, focus, tenacity and a strategic plan.

The developing butterfly egg is enclosed and protected by a hard shell, called chorion, and is lined with a waxy layer that prevents dehydration. It is filled with nutritious fluid that aids the growth of the developing caterpillar. There is a tiny caterpillar on the inside of the egg that is nourished and shielded from the conditions on the outside, which the tiny caterpillar is not yet ready for.

At this stage, while dreams or ideas are still minute and in our heads, we should strive to nurture it. It is important to protect your ideas and to keep them hydrated in order to fuel growth. Having the right mind-set and feeding the mind with positivity helps nourish our dreams and shields them from harsh conditions. The ideal mind-set can help push an idea into action.

A few days after butterfly eggs are laid, a minute, worm-like creature hatches from the egg. The hatching time varies according to the butterfly species and conditions like seasonal temperatures. In addition, the development of the egg can be impacted by other factors like low humidity and the length of daylight hours. Different development strategies may be required to cultivate different dreams and ideas. Some will require longer and more in-depth preparation than

Work out/Engage
What is your unique brand? What are your unique gifts?
Illustration/Aid
Diligent, creative and smart. Researching and organising.

others. The style and length of time will depend on the individual. We all have our unique design.

Embark on something new and discover re-markable things. I am learning to embrace my uniqueness. This involves understanding that my path is going to be unique to me. It may sound obvious that everyone's path is unique, but in a world where there are many conventional ideals and laid down paths for us to follow, we may end up trying to follow someone else's path without carefully thinking about whether this is what we were designed to do.

Some are made to be exceptional artists or great politicians, others remarkable doctors or meticulous accountants. The key is to find what exactly is right for you, what exactly you were designed to do.

Understanding where I fit in this big and ever-buzzing world, I faced a dilemma in trying to figure out what I was uniquely designed to do. From the moment I realised that I did not have to be stuck in a bubble, but rather, I ought to follow the path that is natural to me, a path that is birthed from my passion and involves my gifts and talents. Immediately I realised this; it was as though a spark was ignited within.

A new beginning gives you the opportunity to try something out and discover yourself even further. You can start something new at any age or time. As the quote goes, "The best time to plant a tree was twenty years ago; the next best time is now."

Are you using your gifts and talents? Are you passionate about what you are doing? Are you on the right path for you, or are you putting yourself in a bubble?

As an engineer who appreciates creativity and has a passion for fiction and poetry writing, I admired Debbie Sterling. She is the founder of GoldieBlox, an award-winning, interactive toy company that is mandated to inspire the next generation of female engineers and innovators. I fell in love with her passion, unique communication style, and her ability to combine her love for mathematics and science with her creativity.

I was drawn to her charm and laughed out when she said that in her senior year of high school, her mathematics teacher was writing her a recommendation letter for college and based on her aptitude, advised her to study engineering. Debbie instantly thought, "*No way!* It is boring, intimidating and for boys. It certainly was not for creative and arty people."[7]

She went to Stanford University, decided to give engineering a shot and finally learnt what it was about. She got to invent and design and discovered that "engineering was the skillset to build anything you dream up in your head."

7   Debbie Sterling, "Inspiring the Next Generation of Female Engineers: Debbie Sterling at TEDx-PSU.", TEDX video, April 24, 2013, accessed February 6, 2016, http://tedxtalks.ted.com/video/Inspiring-the-next-generation-2.

As someone who has never felt restricted in making choices about my academics or interests based on my gender, I was inspired by her passion to empower girls to make educational choices based on their aptitude and passion, not their gender.

I selected mathematics, further mathematics, chemistry and physics at A-levels, and I never even considered that STEM (science, technology, engineering and maths) subjects were for boys and not for me. I went on to study engineering, and although there were only a handful of girls in the engineering department, I did not feel like I was not meant to be there.

I believe the girl-child should be given access to quality education and opportunities, given the right support to be all she can be and be allowed to reach for the stars.

As a child, I played with Legos and construction toys. My high-spirited self also loved to roller skate, ride skateboards and play football.

This is why it piqued my interest when the charming Debbie Sterling said that girls like her who did not play with Legos and other construction toys as children because they were traditionally seen as boy toys, have underdeveloped spatial skills and perform worse at spatial skills tests. This puts them at a disadvantage in engineering classes, especially in classes involving three-dimensional drawings.

When Debbie Sterling found out that not playing with construction toys was partly why she struggled with drawing classes that involved three-dimensional drawings at university, it was a light-bulb moment for her. She decided to start something new.

She decided to help the next generation of young girls.

This was a great conception for her as she discovered a need and thought of a great idea to make a construction toy for girls to give young girls the opportunities she did not have.

Debbie Sterling quit her job and went to work. As she went on, she discovered most girls were uninterested in her construction toy prototypes, but they liked books, and they loved to read.

She had another great conception moment! She realised there was a need and she came up with an idea to fill that need by combining *spatial* (construction toys) and *verbal* (stories) to make one toy. It was a toy about a girl engineer named Goldie-Blox who goes on adventures and solves problems by building simple machines. She tested it on many girls, and they loved it.[8]

Even when we get great ideas, there will be challenges of bringing them to fruition. Preparing with suitable conditions and protecting our dream is very important.

Debbie applied to a tech accelerator program, which she did not get into, as they did not understand why she would want to add a book to a construction toy. Undeterred, she took her prototype to the New York toy fair. There, she met with another roadblock. They told her that construction toys for girls do not sell. "It is the way it is." There was not enough belief in her dream.

She felt disappointed, but because she had a dream she believed in, and she had researched and created a tested prototype, she was not willing to give up. The drive did not come solely from having worked on her prototype; it also came from

8   Ibid.

a passion to inspire young girls and let them know they can be engineers and innovators if they want to.

She worked with a factory and turned her prototype into a real toy. There was a minimum of five thousand orders to produce the toy, and she put it on Kickstarter (a funding platform for innovative projects). Her goal was to raise $150,000 in thirty days to make her dream a reality, and she hit her goal in four days.

A personal challenge turned into a "realisation for a need," which transformed from a dream to a prototype and became a reality with more than one million dollars of preorders placed in under a month.

> **Work out/Engage**
>
> *Do you want to embark on something new? What is the purpose of what you are embarking on? What is the value to you and to others?*

Now, GoldieBlox is sold in Toys "R" Us, Amazon and many retailers worldwide.[9]

Prepare inwardly. We get numerous thoughts each day, and good or bad actions usually start with a thought. The thoughts that mostly occupy our mind gradually shape our direction and determine our actions.

What we believe we can or cannot do affects our ability to achieve. Working on our thought processes and beliefs about ourselves is a key part of development. We cannot always prevent thoughts from forming, but we can decide to feed them or not. Actively choose to nurture constructive thoughts.

Realisation and preparation are fundamental to this stage.

9   "GoldieBlox," accessed February 9, 2016, http://www.goldieblox.com/pages/about.

The way you process your dreams and ideas at this stage plays a big part in determining whether your dreams will turn into goals with a strategic plan. How the roots of a plant develop in the soil determines how the plant grows and whether it is firm or easily uprooted. Nurture partly determines whether our plans will be followed through and achieved.

Strong belief and positivity also go a long way. Franklin D. Roosevelt said, "The only limit to our realisation of tomorrow will be our doubts of today." This emphasises how important today is for tomorrow's achievements, as well as the significance of being mentally prepared to achieve our plans in the future.

The first step in the process is realisation. Debbie Sterling discovered a need. Having a great conception starts with realising there is a need for growth, change or an opportunity.

Preparation is the second step. The tiny caterpillar is nourished and prepared inside the butterfly egg until the egg hatches.

A baby prepares and grows inside its mother's womb in favourable conditions for a set period of time before being born. When a child is born prematurely, there are risks of complication, and the baby may need to be supported in an incubator with womb-like conditions.

When a seed is planted, roots start to grow deep inside the soil in favourable conditions before the shoot starts to become visible. The seed is nourished and prepared in the soil to develop a firm anchor and transport system.

Inward preparation is important! There is a similarity in

the processes by which a seed is prepared in the soil, a developing caterpillar is nourished in an egg, a baby grows in the womb, and how our dreams and ideas are first developed in the mind.

For each of these scenarios, we see that the egg, seed and baby are hidden before exposure. There is something about preparing inwardly before exposure. If exposure comes too early, it might result in a disadvantageous, premature experience. There is a certain amount of preparation needed before exposure.

Essentially, the importance of inward preparation in the great conception stage is to develop admirably before the focus that comes with exposure. The condition of the hidden place is designed for our protection and to aid uninterrupted preparation for our next level.

There is power in effective preparation, and this can be seen from nature. Effective preparation helps build a lasting legacy.

If we do not nurture our dreams and visions in our minds adequately, there will be increased risk of complication along the way. The ideal case, which is turning them into set goals and following through, may not happen.

Having a strong belief that we will discover what we are uniquely designed to do, and taking the time and effort to de-

Work out/Engage

Think of three positive things about yourself and what you plan to achieve. Say them to yourself often and speak positivity into what you plan to achieve.

velop ourselves to achieve this, needs a strong foundation that comes from active inward preparation.

Make impact at the conception stage. Conception is an important part of the process. We may be at the beginning of a stage in life, but when we look back at the times we started and completed goals or stages, we can be hopeful for the opportunities of fruition ahead.

We could wonder what the purpose of a fresh start is. It gives the opportunity to build a strong foundation. There are key things to learn and do at that stage that helps support the next stage.

We can add value at the conception stage. Even as we are in the process of discovery, we have a unique factor, which can be utilised to add value and make impact that counts! As Sydney Smith said, "It is the greatest of all mistakes to do nothing because you can only do little—do what you can."

> **Work out/Engage**
>
> *How would you use your uniqueness to make an impact that counts?*

Bottom Line of the Great Conception

Prepare to build a strong foundation. Debbie Sterling showed the power of belief. She was able to push through challenges and concepts that could naturally have killed her dream. She had a determined attitude as she identified the value and impact her dream could have.

This is why the little caterpillar is preparing inside the egg and being nourished because when the egg hatches, the caterpillar is exposed to the conditions of the world outside the egg. Our dreams and ideas are usually protected inside our heads; however, in the process of bringing them to fruition, we risk exposing ourselves and our dreams to many opinions and challenges. It is best to have nurtured them enough in our minds to enable them to stand the test of time.

To follow through in executing our dreams, a focused and determined mind-set is important. Before setting out and acting, take time to prepare mentally.

Develop willpower in the great conception stage. Making New Year's resolutions is a very popular tradition; however, the statistics show that not many people actually stick to their resolution. Statistics show that 45 percent of Americans regularly make New Year's resolutions, and 17 percent infrequently make New Year's resolutions. Although almost half the population in America make New Year resolutions, only 8 percent of people are successful in achieving their resolutions, and 24 percent never succeed and fail on their resolutions each year.[10]

If you have taken time to make resolutions, you probably hope to achieve them. You will be glad to have achieved them by December. So what makes people who were optimistic at the start of the year give up on their resolutions?

Some of the top reasons why people are not successful following through with their New Year resolutions include having unrealistic goals; no plan; lack of mental support to battle

---

10   "New Year's Resolution Statistics. Statistic Brain Research Institute," Statistic Brain, accessed February 10, 2016, http://www.statisticbrain.com/new-years-resolution-statistics/.

doubt, guilt or fear; doing it on their own; lack of support systems; anxiety; wrong perspective; lack of self-belief; reduced willpower; and lack of emotional investment.[11] [12]

About half of the reasons are fully or partly as a result of a mind-set. Determine in your heart that you will succeed, ensure that you continue to strive and remain fully invested.

Know the value of achieving your dreams. A good way of nurturing a dream is by identifying the importance of achieving that dream and knowing the value to you and the world. As the quote goes, "when you do not know the purpose of a thing, you abuse it."

Debbie Sterling saw the value of what she wanted to achieve. Her success will impact the lives of many little girls by building their confidence in problem solving and inspiring the next generation of female engineers and innovators. In addition, Debbie Sterling saw the value to herself, as it would be fulfilling to give a younger generation the opportunity she did not have. This firm awareness of the purpose and value of the fulfilment of a dream helps push us through. These days, people are more health conscious, trying to exercise more, eating healthier and avoiding unhealthy habits like drinking and smoking. Many apps are used to track daily water and calorie intake, steps per day and training data. There is plenty of online information on healthy foods and how to cook easy, healthy meals.

---

11   Jené Luciani. "Top 10 Reasons You Don't Stick to Your Resolutions," SHAPE, accessed February 10, 2016, http://www.shape.com/lifestyle/mind-and-body/top-10-reasons-you-dont-stick-your-resolutions.
12   Emily Rivers, "Top 5 Reasons New Year's Resolutions Fail," The Susquehannock Courier, January 8, 2016, http://shscourier.com/16560/commentary/top-5-reasons-new-years-resolutions-fail/.

For many, wellness has become a day-to-day, active pursuit. It is a daily devotion to exercising and eating right. Health and fitness is one area people are more willing to invest their time and money.

One of the reasons people are becoming more health focused is that they are more aware of the benefits and value of a healthy lifestyle. A lot of research has gone into this area, and there is vast array of easily accessible information on the benefits of living a healthy life.

Someone's vision might be living a healthy life. This could be broken down into goals, such as drinking eight glasses of water a day, eating breakfast every day, consuming five portions of fruits and vegetable a day and exercising three times a week. This is a great vision, and these are amazing goals, but it is one thing to have a dream, and it is another to bring it to fruition.

We have to think of a concrete value. "It will be nice to be healthy" or "Healthy living is what everyone is talking about" might not be strong enough to sustain us when challenges arise. For someone striving for fitness, the ability to keep up with exercising on gloomy days or the willpower to follow through when a scrumptious plate of apple crumble is in sight are two such challenges.

Knowing and thinking of a deeper value to us and others is useful. Healthy living is not just about controlling weight. It helps improves mood, combats diseases, boosts energy and improves longevity. Our families and loved ones will be happier as a result of us being healthy, in the best shape and taking care of ourselves.

Personally, if we are healthy, we feel better, we are more energised and we achieve more. It aids and gives energy for achieving all other goals and aspirations in life more effectively. Recognising this kind of value results in having a firmer resolve to see our hopes come true.

Think of a solid value to yourself and others. Create specific goals with a clear plan within a timeframe like "doing X by Y time through Z activities" to succeed. Acknowledge that it will not be a walk in the park to fulfil your dreams and purpose. There will be challenges; it will take hard work and perseverance. Finally, make a firm decision to stick to it.

The great conception is the foundation for everything else to come. A butterfly egg is immobile, but in its fixed position, it serves as a shield and nourishes the tiny caterpillar inside it. Positive impact on others can be made at any life stage. We can add value even when we are at the smallest point or at humble beginnings. As we make impact on others at this stage, we build ourselves up. There is beauty in small beginnings.

Remember, you are made for a purpose! Keep preparing.

CHAPTER 5

GROWTH: THE CAPACITY BUILDER

The ability to learn is the most important quality a leader can have.

— Sheryl Sandberg

One day, sitting in and enjoying a science class, I learnt about Marie Sklodowska. I was intrigued by this phenomenal lady who, in addition to winning two Nobel Prizes, was the first woman to become a professor at the University of Paris, the Sorbonne. I sat down inspired as I learnt about Marie Sklodowska, famously known as Marie Curie.

Many years later, I found out that she is part of the Curie family legacy of five Nobel Prizes. Some families have received multiple laureates, but the Curie family has received the most Nobel prizes.

Marie Curie received two, in physics and chemistry, and

her husband received the physics prize jointly with her. Her first daughter, Irène Joliot-Curie, was jointly awarded the Nobel Prize in chemistry with her husband, Frédéric Joliot. Henry Labouisse, the husband of Marie Curie's second daughter, *Ève* Curie Labouisse, was the director of UNICEF when it won the Nobel Peace Prize in 1965.[13]

Even though *Ève* Curie did not follow her family's pathway, as she did not choose the career path of a scientist and did not win a Nobel Prize, she did worthwhile work in her lifetime. She achieved degrees in science and philosophy, but her true interests and talents were more musical, artistic, literary, and political than scientific.[14]

Encouraged by her mother, *Ève* developed her skill in music early and performed on many stages across Europe. She worked as a journalist and authored her mother's biography, *Madame Curie*, and a book of war reportage, *Journey among Warriors*.[15] She also committed herself to work for UNICEF, providing help to children and mothers in developing countries.

Marie Curie won her prizes in 1903 and 1911, and till this day, only four people have ever won two Nobel Prizes. In addition to her outstanding achievement, her family has the title of the only family to have received five Nobel Prizes. Even her daughter, who did not go down the science path, still went down as an inspiration in history.

There must have been something special about Marie Cu-

13   "Nobel Prize Facts," NobelPrize.org, http://www.nobelprize.org/nobel_prizes/facts/, accessed February 18, 2016.
14   William L. Hosch, "Ève Curie," Encyclopaedia Britannica, accessed January 19, 2016, http://www.britannica.com/biography/Eve-Curie.
15   "Eve Curie Facts." Biography.yourdictionary.com, accessed January 19, 2016, http://biography.yourdictionary.com/eve-curie.

rie. She had a thirst for knowledge and growth. She understood that living is learning and that it was important to find her unique factor and use it to make a big difference.

Marie Curie was a remarkable woman. Determined to learn, she fought through adversity. Her parents were both teachers, and as a child, Curie took after her father, a math and physics instructor. She had a bright, and curious mind and excelled at school. Unfortunately, at the age of ten, tragedy struck: her mother died.

Even when she became a governess (a woman employed to teach and train children in a private household) after her mother's death because her father could no longer support her, she never lost passion. She continued to study physics, chemistry and mathematics in her spare time to quench her thirst for knowledge.

In 1891, Marie Sklodowska finally made her way to Paris. She enrolled at the Sorbonne, where she studied physics and mathematics. She had naturally discovered a love of the subjects through her unquenchable appetite for learning.

Marie Curie made history in 1903 when she became the first woman to receive the Nobel Prize, winning the prestigious honour in physics along with her husband and Henri Becquerel, for their work on radioactivity. With their Nobel Prize win, the Curies developed a global reputation for their great scientific contributions, and they continued their research.

In 1906, tragedy struck again, and Marie suffered an incredible loss when her husband, Pierre Curie, was killed in

Paris after he accidentally stepped in front of a horse-drawn wagon. Despite her immense grief, Marie took over his teaching post at the Sorbonne, becoming the institution's first female professor.

Marie Curie received another great honour in 1911, winning her second Nobel Prize, this time in chemistry, becoming the first scientist to win two Nobel Prizes. She was selected for her discovery of radium and polonium. While she received the prize alone, she shared the honour jointly with her late husband in her acceptance lecture.

Marie Curie, who has been described as quiet, unassuming and dignified, with a thirst for learning, is held in high esteem and admiration by scientists past and present throughout the world.

Education and culture shape our view of the world. We have extended our view of education over time; we have evolved from seeing education as only academics for a particular gender or occurring only from infancy to coming of age.

We have evolved as a world to value the notion that education is for everyone and that it spans over a large array of subject matters. Art, music, travel, sports—all are part of education, and so is the more formal form, academia. In addition, teaching and learning styles in schools have adapted over time to cater to different types of people.

When we watch toddlers at play, we recognise that learning and growing occur in daily activities. As they play through exploration, games and antics, they discover themselves, learn about their surroundings and start recognising boundaries.

As children play, their imaginations run wild, and their minds expand. They soak in their environments and immerse themselves in their play, and practically everything is a learning experience for them.

Children tend to be curious, easily intrigued and excited by little things. The first day I took my niece and nephew on a train was an adventure. They could hardly sit still. With wide eyes, they glanced left and right, asking several questions and eager to get answers.

Unfortunately, as we grow older, we tend to lose this zeal to soak in our environments, to explore, question and engage. Whilst we may not have such a steep learning curve as children, we should strive to keep learning and growing.

A key to sparkling is to keep learning. What should we know that can further aid our learning and growth?

Everyone has something to offer. Growing up in a family of four girls, I know how similar and different people can be at the same time.

My sisters and I, popularly known as DVees, look very similar; people have said we can pass for quadruplets and it does not help that we all have four-letter names that start with V. I think it is a bit of a stretch until I see a picture of one of us and cannot tell who it is…I sometimes cannot even tell which is me!

With the striking resemblance, we have unique physical features. We react differently to situations emotionally and are affected by different things. That said, we all still cry at each other's birthdays, weddings and many other occasions that call for our tears!

We have distinctive ways of thinking, processing and reacting to the same information. We will solve the same problem in four different ways. Every now and then, as we discuss the same topic, we are equally amazed at how we sometimes think exactly the same thing, and other times we are thinking about it in four distinct ways.

If you take some time to know us well, you discover that even though we have similar mannerisms overall, we also have distinctive personalities with unique idiosyncrasies, passions, gifts and talents.

When we sit at a DVees (a food-and-beverage business that aims to increase the influence of West African food globally) business meeting, each of us brings a unique contribution to the mix; using our own way of thinking, we pick up on and are particular about different things. While one person is more concerned about documentation, the other is more concerned about branding. Whenever we hang out, everyone adds something special to the fun. Voke starts attention-grabbing conversations, Vona rustles up the most delicious food from a fridge that seemed empty, Vese gets up and starts the fun activities and I like to think that I bring happiness to them all.

Everyone has something unique to bring to the table. A collection of who we are, our experiences, personality and talents bring a special flavour that the world is waiting for.

That said, it is beautiful when we can share our thoughts

and respect each other's perspectives. When we think someone is too disadvantaged or deprived to learn from them, we obstruct our opportunity to grow. We can learn something from anyone, regardless of gender, age, class or background.

A man was in a cab that was being driven by a jolly man, quite like Joe, the character from the story I shared in a previous chapter. As the man settled into the cab, he closed his eyes and tried to sleep. He had planned to rest for the entire journey. As the driver tried to start a conversation with him, the man avoided eye contact and refused to encourage a conversation.

This man finally slept, but just as he woke up, his eyes met with the driver's eyes. At this point he had no choice; he reluctantly obliged and struck a conversation with the driver. During the course of their conversation, the cab driver said he wanted to buy a house in England. This piqued the man's interest, and he asked "Would that not be expensive?"

The driver said, "Yes, but I will sell my two houses in Ghana to pay for it. I have three houses in Ghana."

Intrigued now, the man sat up in the car and asked the driver, "How do you do it?"

The driver said, "I save. I kept aside money every month—two hundred pounds, fifty pounds—for two years and bought my plots of land. Then, I saved for two more years and built my houses."

The driver then went on to teach this man about saving plans and how he could cut spending in order to make investments. The man learnt so much and was so inspired that they

Work out/Engage
Think of one or two unlikely people from whom you are going to learn something in the next three months and what you want to learn.
Illustration/Aid
My son, I am going to ask him to teach me basic information about programming and coding." or "My niece, I am going to ask her to teach me a new nursery rhyme."

exchanged phone numbers. The driver promised him that he would check up on him often to ensure he would start his plan.

That was how a man who started a journey with no intention to converse ended up meeting an inspiring driver and acquiring knowledge during a forty-five-minute ride.

I think that the desire and ability to learn, grow and adapt is one of the most attractive qualities in a person. Everyone has something to offer, even if it is just insight from his or her personal experiences. In the most unlikely places, we can find hidden treasure, which can help us grow and unlock our potential.

Constant learning and development is key. The inspirational Nola Ochs is the world's oldest college graduate. She graduated with a 3.7 GPA at the age of ninety-five with her twenty-one-year-old granddaughter!

Her story is astonishing because at ninety-five, one would expect her to want to slow down and reflect on her life, but she saw her long life as an opportunity to take on new challenges and fulfil unattained goals.

At the age of ninety-eight, Nola Ochs received her master's degree, making her the oldest recipient of a master's degree.[16]

---

16   James Klatell, "Meet The 95-Year-Old Graduate," CBSNEWS, May 11, 2007, http://www.cbsnews.com/news/meet-the-95-year-old-graduate/.

When this inspirational woman celebrated her hundredth birthday, she had taken a job as a graduate teaching assistant and was in the process of writing a book.

Nola Ochs is a true inspiration and a testament to the fact that we can keep learning and developing daily. We should not become so comfortable in our way of thinking that we lose the zeal for opportunities to learn more and expand our mind.

Barriers should not hinder our thirst for growth. I have a wonderful aunt who lived with us for many years. She is so sweet and energetic; she has a special song for everyone she knows. I call her wonderful because not only is she very lovely, but I have never met anyone who is as keen to learn as she is.

When I was three or four years old, I was learning phonics and how to read at school. She was so interested in the phonics I was learning that when I came back from school, she would ask me to teach her.

As I grew older, she always made sure I taught her anything interesting that I learnt at school. In her days of learning, subjects were taught differently, and so for her, it was refreshing to learn something from a different generation. We covered subjects from literature to science, mathematics to humanities, and delved into interesting discussions on topics from "the Solar System" to "Factors of Production."

This experience was great for the both of us. Even though I was younger than she was, she felt that I had something to offer from the tender age of four. I never felt too young to add value, and she kept up-to-date and increased her knowledge daily.

Her thirst for knowledge was incredible to watch. She understood the benefits of continuously learning and was determined not to let the barrier of age or background stop her from learning what she could from people.

Growth can also occur by seeking guidance. It helps to consult someone who is more experienced or has vast knowledge in our area of growth, someone who is dependable and willing to give guidance. These more experienced people share wisdom to help us avoid mistakes, help us push through challenges and recover when we do make mistakes. In addition, books can be an excellent source of guidance. We should never stop learning.

> **Work out/Engage**
>
> *Think of something you have always wanted to learn but have made many excuses not to, make a decision to start learning in the next six months. Can you identify more experienced people within an area you are interested in. How can you learn from them?*

caterpillar

Eat and grow like caterpillars. After the butterfly egg hatches, the caterpillar is out in the real world. It is now time for growth.

As we begin discovering who we are, we grow in different areas and gain an awareness of the unique impact we are meant to make. This puts us on a path to make a more specific and significant difference.

As we realise there is a need to find our purpose, the next step is discovery, growing in knowledge and building capacity. Discovering and reflecting on our passions, gifts and strengths is growing in knowledge of ourselves.

As I researched the caterpillar, I fell in love with the purpose of being at the caterpillar stage of a project or in life. In the metamorphosis of the butterfly, this stage is known as the feeding stage, and the mantra in this stage is "Eat and grow."

The hungry little fellow's main purpose is to eat and eat, and as it eats, it grows at an astounding rate. The hatched caterpillar continuously eats from the moment it emerges from the egg. It has been so prepared and is so ready to go that it practically eats its way out of the egg. That puts being proactive on a whole different level!

The caterpillar consumes enough food to survive and sustain itself to adulthood. Without the proper nutrition, the insect may not have the energy to undergo complete transformation, and even if it does, the butterfly may be unable to develop eggs of its own. In the same vein, we should keep learning and increasing in knowledge to ensure we grow to full bloom.

I recall the story of a strong woodcutter who asked a timber merchant for a job, and he got it. The woodcutter was determined to do his very best because the pay and work conditions were great. His boss gave him an axe and showed him the area in the forest where he should work.

The first day, the woodcutter cut down eighteen trees. His boss was extremely impressed and said, "Well done. You are our best woodcutter." Motivated by his boss's words, the woodcutter tried even harder, but by the next day, he only cut down fifteen trees. The third day he tried even harder but only cut down ten trees.

Day after day, the woodcutter cut down fewer and fewer trees. *I must be losing my strength*, the woodcutter thought. He went to the boss and apologised, saying, "I do not understand what is going on."

The boss asked, "When was the last time you sharpened your axe?"

The woodcutter replied, "Sharpen? I have never sharpened my axe. I have been too busy trying to cut down enough trees."[17]

Sometimes we dive into work and get so busy with the work phase that we forget to sharpen our axes and improve ourselves. Knowledge is a great weapon to arm yourself with to get work done effectively.

If you have a desire to develop your character or skill in a certain area, then seek ways to increase knowledge in that area. The theory driving test is a prerequisite to the practical driving test. You prove that you know the rules of the road before showing that you can be an effective driver. If I want to improve my leadership skills, I will read books on leadership and research and understudy great leaders. Then, I will begin

---

17   Stephen, "The Story of a Woodcutter," Motivation, accessed March 3, 2016, http://academictips. org/blogs/the-story-of-a-woodcutter/.

to act out what I have learnt. Although it is possible to learn based on your own experiences, understudying others who have achieved what you want can help ease the process.

My mother is remarkable. She studied economics at the University of Lagos in Nigeria. After she graduated in 1979, she completed her National Youth Service Corps (NYSC, which is set up by the Nigerian government to involve the nation's graduates in the development of the nation) at Central Bank of Nigeria. At twenty-three, she started on a graduate scheme and proceeded to work for NICON Insurance in Lagos, Nigeria. My mother acquired her professional qualification, Associate of Chartered Insurance Institute (ACII), in 1990 and focused on becoming an expert in her field. After twenty-six years of a successful career, she decided it was time to retire.

I have always known my mum loved children, and it was her dream and a passion of hers to own a school one day. I saw her at the stage of her retirement and watched as she recalled this dream.

My mother knew that the realisation of her dream would add value to others, which would be the chance to impact young children with good and wholesome values as well as to nurture future leaders.

She enrolled in courses to learn about child day care. She learnt about the stages of childhood, social issues and family support. I watched as my mother continuously studied and re-searched about babies, toddlers, learning styles, perfect learn-ing tools, toys as well as how to create a school motto and run a school.

My mum went through the capacity-builder stage; she increased in knowledge and built capacity. For her dream to stand the test of time, she had to have the right nutrition (knowledge) and be proactive so her dream could grow to its adult phase. Then she started the school.

I have seen my mum push through to fulfil her dreams and overcome challenges. She has been running D-Vees School for nine years now, fulfilling her purpose, impacting the next generation and developing leaders of tomorrow. Needless to say, I am so proud of my mother.

Discovering our purpose is not enough. We need to educate ourselves and build capacity for the work involved.

Building capacity and increasing in knowledge go hand in hand. A caterpillar can grow one hundred times larger or more after it emerges from the egg because of its constant feeding.

As the caterpillar eats, it grows so much that it becomes too big for its skin. This exceptional growth rate means that caterpillar skins are soon stretched until they are unable to expand any more. When this point is reached, the caterpillar grows a new skin underneath the outer skin. It sheds the old skin, and the newer, larger skin, which is capable of accommodating further growth, is displayed. The caterpillar gets more capacity to consume more food and to grow larger.

As we increase in knowledge and learning, we need to enlarge our capacity because we will become bigger than our current state or space. We continue to learn, grow and increase knowledge and ability at an exceptional rate that we become stretched and will need to increase capacity to house further growth.

Increased capacity is not only implied physically; it also applies spiritually, mentally, emotionally, financially and more.

A new capacity level gives us the ability to understand and fulfil a specific function in alignment with the capacity we have; however, sometimes we have more ability for growth, but we refuse to enlarge our capacity.

We can build capacity by stretching ourselves, setting new goals and putting ourselves in situations that will help us grow.

A lady who lived in fear finally started a beginner's swimming class after many attempts. She had been in the beginner's class for a year and had been performing on an intermediate level; however, she refused to go to the intermediate class because of fear. Her instructor was frustrated that she was limiting her growth and said, "This class is too small for you, but you refuse to progress. I cannot teach you beyond what you know here because this is no longer the right place for you."

She had grown beyond her current stage or level but refused to enlarge her space and thus build more capacity.

For the caterpillar, the newly revealed skin is usually very soft. With time, the new skin hardens and moulds itself to the caterpillar. When we

> **Work out/Engage**
>
> *What knowledge or skill do you need for where you are going that you do not currently have, and what are you going to do about it? How are you going to step outside your comfort zone to stretch yourself and build capacity?*

make room for growth, it is normal to sometimes feel out of our depth at first. It might seem like we are threading unfamiliar paths, but with time and perseverance, we become more confident.

Consume the right nutrition. We should have an appetite to consume knowledge the way caterpillars eat; however, although caterpillars are eating machines, they are particular about what they eat.

The caterpillar is so particular about what it eats that the butterfly is careful to lay its eggs on the specific leaf it should consume upon hatching.

While it is possible to learn something new from everyone we meet, sometimes we have to go out to seek specific information. This specific knowledge should be tailored to what we aim to achieve. This helps with focus as the right nutrition is needed to push through to the next stage.

During my period of growth (of breaking out of restrictive shyness), I realised just how vital the "eat and growth" phase was and the power of consuming the right information. I always thought that part of being an introvert was natural shyness, a part of my personality.

Hardly anyone is a complete introvert or extrovert, as most people are on a scale ranging from introvert to extrovert, manifesting qualities of each, depending on the circumstance; however, I identify as being more on the introvert side of the spectrum.

I enjoy the simple pleasures of being at home. Being able

to come home, change into comfortable clothes and eat while watching the best TV shows is bliss. I appreciate little quirks like experimenting with cooking, dancing in front of my mirror for hours and how I love the comfort of my bed while enjoying a good book.

Although I knew I was more of an introvert than extrovert, I had some misconceptions about it and assumed that being bashfully shy was normal for introverts and somehow part of the package.

As I began to increase my knowledge on the topic, a Ted Talk, "The Power of Introverts" by Susan Cain, led to more understanding on the importance of having the right information being fed into our minds.

Susan Cain says, "Being an introvert is different from being shy. Shyness is the fear of social judgement while introversion is more about how you respond to stimulation including social stimulation." The traits can overlap; although scientists tend to debate to what degree.

Things are not always in absolute; however, generally, extroverts crave large amounts of stimulation, and introverts feel more alive and the most capable when they are in quieter environments. By having the right information, I started seeing being an introvert in a new, refreshing light. I realised I could be an introvert without the limiting shyness. It was *not* part of the package.

I had been aware of some of the strengths of extroverts and introverts but never really looked deeply into the strength of both personality types, their unique contributions to society and the science behind them.

Research brought to light why, even though all the tests said I was more on the introvert side of the spectrum and I identified as one, I did not totally feel like one. Some of the things I thought were introvert behaviour were overthinking, being shy, being unemotional and disliking talking and working in groups. In addition, I assumed introverts did not like socialising, were poor at public speaking and did not make good leaders.

The above categorisation confused me because a lot of it did not apply to me holistically, and it mainly depended on my environment. I was generally shy, but I could be either really quiet or converse comfortably, depending on a range of factors, including the environment and my passion or interest in the topic.

Meaningful and relaxed one-on-one or small group conversations make me feel alive and engaged, even though I may be silent in a large group of people. I enjoy concerts and social interactions and experiences, but not excessively. Family time is very important to me, and I will spend the bulk of my time with family, but I also love quiet time every now and then as both settings help me relax.

The misconception of detesting group work also confused me. Group work is interesting for me, as I love learning from others and observing how different people work, but I also enjoy working on my own as well because I am at my most creative and switched on when I am working alone and in a quiet environment.

The book *Introvert Advantage: How Quiet People Can Thrive in an Extrovert World* by Marti Olsen Laney, as well as further research, suggests that there is science behind personality types that is really interesting.

Studies show that introversion and extroversion are partially based on how individual brains function. Through brain-imaging technology, researchers suggest that the way introverts' and extroverts' brains process information is different.

Science suggests that introverts' blood flows through a more complex and internally focused path in the brain and increases in the parts of the brain associated with memory, planning and problem-solving processes. It suggests that for introverts, it takes the brain longer to complete a thought. This may be why introverts appear to take more time to process information but tend to give more reflective and analytical responses. Introverts have a reflective nature and are clearer about ideas and thoughts once they have had time to process them.

Extroverts' blood flows through a shorter path, and it flows to the areas of the brain where visual, auditory, touch and taste sensory processing occurs. And as such, extroverts respond to stimuli much quicker. They process thoughts faster, which is why they are quick on their feet.[18] Extroverts get energised by social interactions, tend to formulate their ideas best by articulating them and generally think quickly on their feet.

The pathway of the blood flow is not about intelligence;

18   D. L. Johnson, J. S. Wiebe, S. M. Gold, N. C. Andreasen, R. D. Hichwa, L. Watkins, and L. L. Boles Ponto, "Cerebral Blood Flow and Personality: A Positron Emission Tomography Study," The American Journal of Psychiatry 156 no. 2 (1999): 252–257.

it is basically about how both personality types process and retrieve information.[19]

I discovered that I had misconstrued things. Consuming the right knowledge for my development helped me understand both personalities better, why people think and respond differently. Both types have something unique to offer, and every personality had its strengths and weaknesses. It is the ability to build on and utilise the strengths, manage the weaknesses effectively and appreciate differences in people that matters.

I saw that both personality types have a lot to contribute to leadership and creativity.[20] The tasks a leader has to undertake may come more naturally to some than others but any personality type could make a good leader if they develop certain skills.

One of the quotes from *Lean In* by Sheryl Sandberg that really stuck was: "True leadership stems from individuality that is honestly and sometimes imperfectly expressed. Leaders should strive for authenticity over perfection."

The key is to understand ourselves, embrace who we are and express what we have to offer in our own special way. When we go against the core of who we were designed to be, we deplete ourselves and what we uniquely bring to the table. It is more about being our best, authentic self and giving things our best shot rather than perfection.

While we may express ourselves in an imperfect way, we are undergoing a process. True leadership is attainable if I

19   Marti Olsen Laney, The Introvert Advantage: How Quiet People Can Thrive in an Extrovert World (Workman Publishing Company, 2002), Kindle location 786.
20   Susan Cain, "The Power of Introverts," TED video, February 2012, accessed February 10, 2016, https://www.ted.com/talks/susan_cain_the_power_of_introverts?language=en.

learn to be my best self and build solid character. The key is to keep working towards developing myself daily and thriving to be all I was designed to be.

Without coming across the research and books I mentioned above, my mind and its capacity would not have expanded in such a way. I consumed the right knowledge for me, which in turn enlarged the scope of my vision. It also brought about a stronger desire in me to keep learning. I enlarged

> **Work out/Engage**
>
> *Review your learning materials. Are they fulfilling their purpose and leading you the right way? If not, why?*

the capacity of my mind, and I believe this is a vital purpose of this stage.

Bottom Line of the Capacity Builder

Thirst for knowledge and commit to development. With all her amazing, mind-blowing achievements, there are three beautiful quotes by the outstanding Marie Curie that make her story even more remarkable. She had a profound insight and way of thinking.

The first quote is, "You cannot hope to build a better world without improving the individuals. To that end each of us must work for his own improvement, and at the same time share a general responsibility for all humanity, our particular duty being to aid those to whom we think we can be most useful."

This is very apt as it reiterates the point that for the world to be a better place, we all need to play our part of developing ourselves. The latter has even more depth as it expresses that the ultimate goal is not to develop ourselves just for our own enjoyment but also to make a difference in other people's lives and impact in the world.

That is what the sparkle process is about. We learn and grow to make a difference. We build up ourselves to build a city. We develop capacity to make impact. Marie Curie understood that changing the world started with changing ourselves. She believed that the end goal was to be useful and effective.

Also stated by Marie Curie: "Life is not easy for any of us. But what of that? We must have perseverance and above all confidence in ourselves. We must believe that we are gifted for something and that this thing must be attained."

Marie Curie understood that achieving our goals will come with challenges. We have to believe in ourselves and persevere to achieve what we were designed for. She believed that everyone has been given special gifts for a unique purpose.

Finally, Marie Curie understood process: "I was taught that the way of progress was neither swift nor easy."

These quotes reiterate the great conception—capacity builder—remarkable change—blossomed fulfilment—ripple effect process. Believe in yourself or dream or purpose (newness), work to develop and thirst for knowledge (growth), persevere and work hard (transformation), attain what you have been gifted for (fruition) and be useful (impact). Marie Curie had certain beliefs, and she went on to have some of the most phenomenal achievements in history.

Develop a growth strategy. Caterpillars are very creative in protecting themselves from predators and resourceful in their self-defence. Some caterpillars, such as the early instars of black swallowtails, look like bird droppings, and certain inchworms imitate twigs to prevent themselves from being preyed on.

Other caterpillars practise a different and contrary strategy, making themselves noticeable with vivid colours to publicise their toxicity. Some go the extra mile in their strategy by using thanatosis. They fall to the ground and play dead when touched in an attempt to frustrate the predator's efforts. We need to develop a strategy to survive through the challenges that will come along the way as we desire to learn, grow and build capacity. It will not be an easy process; it helps to be strategic. Have a game plan and proposed action for growth! Create a master plan and blueprint for survival! Be inspired by the caterpillar. It feeds and grows effectively to make it to its next stage and to keep the insect surviving even when it is a butterfly.

Understanding the purpose of the capacity builder. The caterpillar might dislike its level in the stages of the butterfly; however, it has been equipped to survive the challenges of being a caterpillar.

As time goes on, I learn more about being an effective introvert; I read, listen to audios, watch videos, try to give talks. Although it would have been nice to wake up one day and have all the restrictive parts of shyness be gone, I know there is a reason for the process.

I am meant to be growing in knowledge, building capacity

while helping others. I have to make a conscious effort to not let the challenges of still being in this stage, like the fear of freezing when giving a presentation, prevent me from attempting. I learn strategy from different sources like "10 Public Speaking Tips from My Year of Speaking Dangerously"[21] and "How to Be Heard When You Aren't the Loudest Voice in the Room."[22]

It is a constant reminder that when we have increased in knowledge and grown, we have to build more capacity for even more growth. It is being able to accept and be at ease with the fact that we may not be where we want to be in a certain area, but the right progress is being made, and we are doing all we can and making impact in the way we can at this stage.

The key is to seek the right nutrition by finding the appropriate source of knowledge and way to learn and by learning from the right people.

The capacity builder is the treasure of the process. Growing into our uniqueness and what we have been called to do through learning and discovery is key. The caterpillar has four or five parts to its growth stage, called instars. It is a step-by-step process, and this shows that even as rapid growth is vital, pace and process are also important. It is a continuous, almost cyclical process of learn and build capacity.

Remember, you are able! Keep learning and growing.

---

21   "10 public speaking tips from my year speaking dangerously", Quiet Revolution, Susan Cain, accessed February 20, 2016, http://www.quietrev.com/10-public-speaking-tips-from-my-year-of-speaking-dangerously/
22   "How to be heard when you aren't the loudest voice in the room", Quiet Revolution, Meagan Francis, accessed Fenruary 20, 2016, http://www.quietrev.com/how-to-be-heard-when-you-arent-the-loudest-voice-in-the-room/

CHAPTER 6

TRANSFORMATION: THE REMARKABLE CHANGE

Just when the caterpillar thought the world was over...it became a butterfly.

— Unknown

Big changes require patience.

— Unknown

How beautiful is transformation? With time, it turns a crawling caterpillar into a flying butterfly. Transformation takes and uses what we currently have to further bring out our beauty through a process.

My academic transformation started when my mother spoke to a teacher. I used to perform well at school, not top of my class good but decent. Then I got to year four in primary school, and I was struggling.

I had been away from school for a month, and when I came back, I had missed quite a lot. I could not understand what we were doing in mathematics and other subjects. The teacher had taught highest common factor (HCF) and lowest common multiple (LCM) in mathematics while I was away, and when I got back, I found it difficult to understand these factors and multiples. I started getting terrible grades in mathematics that term. I recall scoring zero on a class exercise once. This event was followed by being shamed publicly by my teacher, and she stated that I was performing behind the class. The teacher's statement sowed a seed of doubt in my abilities, and I began to believe that perhaps I was not that bright. I thought, *Maybe I am terrible at mathematics*. This is why at eight, I would have laughed out loud if I was told I would one day score 100 percent in mathematics effortlessly, or that I would graduate with a first-class engineering degree.

The teacher was unable to see the diamond that was waiting to be mined. She mentioned to my mother that I was struggling and that she was considering moving me from the top class to the bottom class. Her words were clear: "She is not good at mathematics and is struggling in year four."

My mother said she thought, *My child is not average*, and her desire to let me know this fact prompted her to speak with me. My mother called me one lovely evening. One look at her face, and I knew it was going to be a serious conversation. She said, "Do not believe that you are average. Do not be comfortable being mediocre." Those words sit in my mind till today.

My mother was concerned; she knew that although I had not been performing exceptionally well in my academics, I had never failed at school. She reckoned that there had to be a reason for the recent decline in my performance. She knew I had abilities, an analytical mind and the ability to pick things up quickly. She recognised that I had logical gifts that were not being harnessed.

She felt that it was important for me to know that I was not average, and that the problem was more associated with me needing someone who was patient enough to explain what I missed in class. My mother decided to get me a tutor to do just that.

Different people have different types of intelligence. Some are more artistic, some musical, some number smart, some word smart and so many others. Some people will be skilled dancers; others will be exceptional designers or powerful speech deliverers or political giants. Unknown to me at that time, I was gifted with numbers.

I started with a tutor when I turned nine. He was a fantastic teacher and was patient enough to bring out the sparkle in me. His job was to teach me, but he surpassed the expectation of what he was required to do. He somehow sparked my interest in mathematics and made me see that it came easily to me. He explained what I did not understand and made me see that I was actually very skilled with numbers.

Within a short time, the effects started to show. For the first time, I started to get excited at the thought of having extra tutoring. I was eager to tackle one hundred mathematics questions a day, three times a week at the age of nine. I was so keen on learning, and within a month, I started scoring the highest in mathematics and math-related subjects in my class. It was the words from my mother and tutor that fuelled my belief that I could be exceptional in my academics, and this soon reflected in my performance in other subjects. The more comfortable and confident I became with numbers, the better I performed at other subjects. Teachers started calling me "the ever-improving Vome." I started from not being in the top twenty in my year, to moving up to the twelfth position, to the sixth, and then finishing as one of the top three students. Teachers marvelled!

The day I finished primary school, a parent told my mother, "Vome just took all the class prizes." This was a serious transformation from "She is not good at mathematics and is struggling generally" to "Vome is exceptional with numbers and should represent the class in academic competitions."

From then on, I went on passionately loving mathematics. From the day I left primary school until my graduation from university, I achieved top marks (perfect score on many occasions) in every mathematics exam or test I took. I look back now and realise that the string of achievements started from an observation my mother made and was brought to fruition by a tutor who did his job excellently. My mother saw that although her daughter appeared to be struggling now, her child had logical and creative abilities that she could see. She discovered the diamond that was in me, and my tutor did the cutting and polishing, which involved almost three hundred mathematics questions a week until that diamond was ready.

We all have different gifts inside us. Sometimes all we need is to see beyond our present state, identify the value in us, and we embark on the journey to cut and polish that gift in order to bring out its full splendour. Transformation is a journey.

The caterpillar does not know it has potential to be a butterfly until one day it gets wrapped up in a chrysalis, and the transformation begins. What should we know about transformation?

Transformation requires resolve. We cannot emerge a butterfly without change, and bringing dreams to fruition comes with hard work that involves sacrifice. Undergoing self-discovery, developing ourselves, discovering our purpose and going for it with determination all come with their own trials.

The ability to be willing to be objective and look into ourselves is essential; we may find things we like and also find things we do not like. We need to be able to deal with the negatives and strengthen the positives. We need the ability to work hard to reach the desired end goal, even when we do not feel like working.

Some people embrace change, and some are less comfortable with this unfamiliar word called "change." There is a story of a girl who complained to her father that her life was miserable, and she did not know how she was going to get by. She was tired of challenges, of constantly fighting and struggling. It seemed as one problem was solved, another one followed.

Her father took her to the kitchen, filled three pots with water and placed each on a fire. Once the three pots began to boil, he placed potatoes in one pot, eggs in the second and ground coffee beans in the third. He let them sit and boil without saying a word to his precious daughter. The girl impatiently waited, wondering what he was doing.

After some minutes he turned off the burners, took the potatoes out of the pot and placed them in a bowl, pulled the eggs out and placed them in a bowl and ladled the coffee out and placed it in a cup. Turning to his daughter he asked, "Daughter, what do you see?"

"Potatoes, eggs, and coffee," she hastily replied.

"Look closer," he said. "Touch the potatoes." She did and noted that they were soft. He asked her to take an egg and break it. After pulling off the shell, she observed the hard-boiled egg. Finally, he asked her to sip the coffee. Its rich aroma brought a smile to her face.

"Father, what does this all mean?" she asked.

He explained that the potatoes, the eggs and coffee beans had each faced the same adversity—the boiling water; however, each one reacted differently.

The potato went in strong, hard and unrelenting, but in boiling water, it became soft and weak. The egg was fragile, with the thin outer shell protecting its liquid interior, until it was put in the boiling water, and the inside of the egg became hard. The ground coffee beans were unique. After they were exposed to boiling water, they changed the water and created something rich and new.

"Which are you?" he asked his daughter. "When adversity knocks on your door, how do you respond? Are you a potato, an egg, or a coffee bean?"[23]

In life, change is inevitable; things happen around us, and to us, but what truly matters is what happens within us and what we do with this change.

Physically, we experience change in our bodies as we grow, stop growing and start to age. Our thought process changes over time based on what our mind consumes and is exposed to. Situations change around us, and life as we know it can suddenly transform.

We undergo varied changes, and in order to be our best selves, we need to work at changing for the better and improving ourselves each day in different ways—our *skills, character, knowledge*.

This stage is the work and transformation stage, and it has its own conditions, function and purpose. This is the phase of making it happen; it requires resourcefulness, dedication and patience to get through.

In many situations, change will not happen immediately, and work will not give the desired results in an instant. In a lot of situations, making a change or working towards fulfilling a dream comes with all sorts of tests and challenges; however, our dreams should be bigger than the challenges. Focusing on our desired end goal and the value it will bring can help make

23   "Struggles of our life" mstories, accessed March 8, 2016, http://www.moralstories.org/struggles-of-our-life/

our dreams appear bigger than the inevitable challenges on the way.

Sometimes we get tired, anxious and stressed. Times come when we have no drive to go on. Mistakes are made along the way; we are critical and hard on ourselves. We fear that we are not progressing as fast as we should, and then we get frustrated for not moving faster. People let us down; people hurt us. The busyness of life distracts us and takes over. We let ourselves down, and life happens.

Our desire to be and to do what we have been purposed to do pushes and strengthens us to go through some of the most surprising circumstances.

Sometimes we do not even realise how strong we are until we have to show such resilience. Challenges are definitely not easy...but they help shape us by building our strength and character. The absence of trials in life is unrealistic. It is the ability to go through these trials with grace, to learn to fulfil the purpose of that storm, and come out strong that brings beauty out of the struggle. If you decide to stretch yourself, challenges are inevitable.

Sheryl Sandberg said, "The ability to forge a unique path with occasional dips, detours, and even dead ends presents a better chance for fulfilment." Occasional dips, detours and even dead ends will come along the way, but we can learn something as a result of pushing through. You might discover that you are really stronger than you thought you were, or you could discover purpose from your pain.

We do not always get it right the first time. Sometimes we fail, but making it to fruition requires possessing the ability to identify the mistake, to correct it and start over with the determination to conquer. I evolved from

Work out/Engage
Have you failed at something recently? What led to it? How can you correct it? What did you learn from the experience? What would you do differently next time?
Illustration/Aid
Started a business that collapsed. Hired the wrong people and I did not know enough about the business.

seeing failure as a dead end to realising that it is a learning opportunity. I started seeing it as a weapon that made me stronger and wiser. I do not hope to fail, but if I do fall, I hope to pick myself up with value added.

John C. Maxwell said, "A man must be big enough to admit his mistakes, smart enough to profit from them, and strong enough to correct them."

All our experiences contribute to making us who we are. Use them to do something good and make an impact.

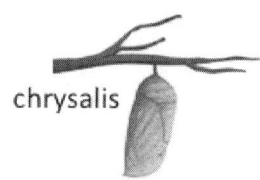

chrysalis

Step by step, day by day, not an overnight process.
It is in the chrysalis stage that the most remarkable change happens.

After the caterpillar is done growing, a chrysalis (a protective container) forms in which the caterpillar changes into a striking butterfly. In the chrysalis, the caterpillar tissues break down, limbs and organs of the caterpillar transform and the butterfly structures start forming.

During transformation, habits we want to change should start dropping off as new, desired habits start forming. If I desire to be more generous, the less I think about my needs and more attentive I become to the needs of others, the more I will be compelled to help.

The remarkable thing about this stage is that when the insect is in the chrysalis, it could look like nothing is going on from the outside, but big changes are occurring on the inside. Special cells that were present in the caterpillar are now growing quickly and will become the legs, antennae, wings, eyes and other parts of the adult butterfly.

Most times when we are in the process of working towards a change, it could look like progress is barely being made, but big changes are occurring inside of us. Keep putting in the work!

The original caterpillar cells will provide energy for the growing butterfly cells. In the same way, the knowledge we have gained and capacity we have built in the previous stage will provide drive and support for the work and transformation.

Transformation occurs day by day, step by step, but each step speaks volumes. We should push through with each step, as we remember to drop the negatives and pick up the positives.

As I worked towards growing and developing, I built my knowledge and tried building my capacity by putting myself out of my comfort zone, and the changes started from within. I started by seeing being an introvert differently; then my mindset started changing, and the possibilities I had opened up to myself expanded. My thinking was getting renewed, and even though, externally, it did not look like many changes were occurring, there were big changes going on internally.

Eyes are on the vivid butterfly as it flies by. In the chrysalis stage, the insect is hidden, and there is no constant focus. What makes the butterfly survive this new constant attention (chances of being preyed on) are the key changes that occur in the chrysalis.

From observation, I notice that usually, when I accomplish something, the challenges I went through on the way to the end goal were somehow preparing me for when that accomplishment happened.

From research, it can be noticed that the challenges that many great people in history experienced and the lessons learnt during those times were somehow preparing and positioning them to attain their greatness. Most times, it seems the challenges help us grow to a place where we can carry the effects of the fulfilment of our goal with more grace.

If the same thing was accomplished earlier without overcoming some of the challenges, we may not fully value the importance of what we accomplished, or we may not be fully prepared to handle it.

For different projects and individuals, the length of time required to stay at this stage will vary. There are certain goals achievable in a few weeks, and some take years. There are changes I have been able to make in months and some I am still working on. Some people will spend a longer time on achieving a particular goal than others and will spend less time on some. It is all relative! We just have to make sure we are not working too fast or too slowly for our unique design and pace.

Work out/Engage
What one step are you going to take towards your desired change?

The capacity builder and the remarkable change stages sometimes go together in a cycle before we reach our end goal. A lot of times, the process goes thus: increase knowledge and learn—build capacity—make changes. And then the cycle repeats itself until we are where we want to be. This is because change is usually a process that requires continuous effort and renewal of mind.

Direction can be changed. We can start to change our story at the point we realise that we do not like our direction. The quote goes, "we may not have had a good start, but we can have a great finish." We can go back to the drawing board. We can go back to the great conception.

It is a rare man who gets to read his own obituary. Alfred Nobel was the Swedish scientist, entrepreneur and industrialist who is famous for using his vast fortune to establish the Nobel

Prize, which is known for awarding the greatest achievements throughout the world. The foundation of the Nobel Prize honours people from all around the world for their great accomplishments in physics, chemistry, medicine, literature, and for work in peace.

As a young man, Alfred Nobel worked at his father's factory. He was a very intellectually curious young man who experimented with chemistry and explosives. Alfred Nobel dedicated himself to the study of explosives.

His brother Emil was killed in a tragic accident in a nitroglycerine explosion. Alfred Nobel was particularly interested in the safe manufacture and use of nitroglycerine, a highly unstable explosive. He incorporated nitroglycerine into silica, an inert substance, which made it safer and easier to manipulate. He patented it in 1867 with the name "dynamite."

Dynamite established Nobel's fame and was soon widely used in mining internationally. Nobel went on to invent a number of other explosives. His inventions helped him attain a great deal of wealth.[24]

After Alfred's brother Ludvig died in Cannes in 1888, a French newspaper mistakenly published Alfred's obituary instead of Ludvig's, stating that "the merchant of death is dead" and condemning him for his invention of dynamite. Alfred was saddened to realise that this was how he would be remembered after his death, as he was a pacifist at heart.[25]

He did not want to be remembered as the reason behind

---

24   "Alfred Nobel," Biography.com, accessed January 20, 2016, http://www.biography.com/people/alfred-nobel-9424195.
25   Ibid.

mass destruction. He left the major portion of his wealth for the creation of the Nobel Prize to honour and award eminence in five different fields: physics, chemistry, medicine, literature and work in peace. An economics prize was later established by Sweden's central bank, Sveriges Riksbank, in 1968 in honour of Alfred Nobel.

Alfred Nobel, who had a slightly controversial reputation, turned it around significantly. Whether that was his intention or not is a matter up for debate, but he was able to do this through the establishment of the Nobel Prize. He is now well known for using his wealth to honour men and women who have done excellently in their fields with one of the most honourable awards a person can get.

One of the fields is a prize for work in peace. A man who was well known for inventing dynamite and other explosives is now better known for honouring people who have done the most or the best work for fraternity between nations, the abolition or reduction of standing armies and for the holding and promotion of peace congresses for their work in peace.[26]

> **Work out/Engage**
>
> *Consider this in different areas of your life. Do you like the direction you are going in? What do you think will be said about you when you are gone? If you do not like both, what can you do to change your story?*

Not everyone will have the rare opportunity of seeing what will be said about them when they are gone. It might not be possible to make corrections based on that rare opportunity, but if we realise we are

---

walking in a wrong direction, we can switch lanes. Realising we are on an unideal path and changing direction may not be easy, but it can be done. We can change our story!

Get support. In some motorsports, a racing car stops in the pits for refuelling, change of tyres, repairs and mechanical adjustments. Although the racer is the main person in the race, he or she needs support to make it to the finish line. Similarly, we need motivators, supporters, encouragers and accountability systems to help us reach our finish line smoothly.

The desire to achieve a goal might be there, but if there is nothing to keep us motivated and accountable, the chance of failure is higher. We need the right motivation around us to make our dream a reality.

During the stage of work and transformation, it is important to guard our minds and bodies from getting weary and giving up. Change is not easy. We need a proper covering that protects the goals that we are working towards from harsh conditions (challenges) which can deter us from fulfilment.

It helps at this stage to have people who will be able to motivate us to make those key changes, people who will support us and give us honest feedback on how we are progressing, people who are willing to encourage us even when every fibre in our body is screaming, *"No!"* We should surround ourselves with people who will support our process and allow us blossom.

Motivation and encouragement come in different forms. Not everyone will need a football team of people to achieve every dream. For some people, it is that one person who believes in them and helps them pull through making difficult changes or work towards a goal. Some others have a team of people cheering them on in the right direction.

Our faith and a deep desire in us to make a difference is a solid motivator and source of encouragement. My faith in God has been essential and indispensable in getting me through the process that is life. It has served as a significant source of motivation, encouragement and support and has helped me flourish in good times and also navigate challenging times. My family has been a great source of motivation and strong support system. Those have been my source of support both in great and tough times.

Another source of motivation could be thinking about why we started this journey in the first place. This is why what was done in the great conception stage, thinking of the value of what we want to achieve to others and to ourselves, is vital.

During the season of work, thinking about the value of what we are aiming for and the impact we want to make can push us through and remind us that what we are doing is bigger than us and will have a positive effect on others. We all need drive to keep us going, to help us

> **Work out/Engage**
>
> *How do you keep yourself accountable in order to make sure you follow through with your goals? If you do not have one or your current method is not working, how can you put an effective accountability structure in place?*

through difficulties and discouragement.

Bottom Line of the Remarkable Change

Get motivation, support and accountability systems. Richard Williams was a key helper in his children's lives. Not only did he have a dream for his daughters and a thorough plan to accomplish that dream for their lives, he increased his knowledge and improved skills to make it happen. A father's dream was birthed. The Williams sisters, Venus and Serena Williams, play professional tennis.

Venus Williams has been ranked number one in the world in singles by the Women's Tennis Association on three separate occasions and has won the singles Grand Slam title seven times.

Serena Williams is ranked number one in women's singles tennis; the Women's Tennis Association has ranked her number one in the world in singles on six separate occasions, and she has won the singles Grand Slam title twenty-two times. They are both sports legends.

Their father, Richard Williams, was at home one day, watching television when he started watching a tennis match. Williams watched in astonishment as he found out that the player won a lot of money for four days' work in relation to winning a tennis tournament. Richard Williams then made up his mind that his children would play tennis.

This dream was far from realistic as Venus and Serena were not born yet, and he did not know how to play tennis; however, self-motivation and determination encouraged him. Richard Williams wrote a seventy-eight-page plan mapping out how he was going to achieve his dream for his unborn daughters, and he read and learnt all he could about tennis[27].

Richard William became an avid fan of tennis and envisioned his daughters as champions even before they were born. Their family moved to Compton, a suburb of Los Angeles, California, when Venus and Serena were very young. This move was not by chance; he moved to Compton because he felt that was the best place for his daughters to grow up and get a fighter's mentality[28].

He used what he gleaned from tennis books and videos to instruct Serena and Venus on how to play the game. Both Serena and Venus showed promise at a very early age, prompting their outspoken father to begin making predictions about their future success in the tennis world.

They were both coached by their father and excelled in highly competitive tournaments. By 1991, Serena was 46-3 on the junior United States Tennis Association tour and ranked first in the 10-and-under division.[29] By the age of ten, Venus' serve topped one hundred miles per hour, a weapon she used to go 63-0 on the United States Tennis Association junior tour.[30]

Richard Williams dreamed that his daughters would be number one, and he instilled confidence, courage and commitment in them to believe they could achieve their dreams and be determined to do it. He was determined to do the work to make his daughters into tennis champions. They were determined to do the work…and something remarkable happened!

27   Richard William and Bart Davis, Black and White: The way I see it (Atria)
28   Ibid.
29   "Serena Williams," Biography.com, accessed March 9, 2016 http://www.biography.com/people/serena-williams-9532901#related-video-gallery.
30   "Venus Williams," Biography.com, accessed March 9, 2016 http://www.biography.com/people/venus-williams-9533011.

The Williams sisters went through the intense work to get to fruition and they had their father guiding them through. He kept them accountable; he coached them, motivated them and helped them go through challenges.

We need real motivators, encouragers and helpers, and they come in all shapes, forms and sizes.

Be dedicated to the transformation. Becoming successful in any aspect of life requires dedication. Be confident that you have been designed for a special purpose, and you can make those changes and do the work to fulfil purpose. Believe that you are able. Do not be discouraged; we can withstand and conquer. Big changes will happen, starting from within. The process of evolving is not always easy but we can grow and become better versions of ourselves. No one really thinks about the drastic change the butterfly has undergone to achieve its specific beauty. Be dedicated to the process of bringing the desired outcome to fruition.

Take a step in the right direction. Not everything will be within our control, but we can start with little. We can take a first step in the right direction and gradually build up. We often make the mistake of thinking that we need to take huge steps to make a change. Even a minuscule step in the right direction makes a huge difference as it puts us in a better position than before that tiny step was taken. Use the tools of motivation, encouragement and dedication to take the step towards transformation, and even though you lack some of the tools, take the step anyway. If you discover that you are walking in the wrong direction, take a U-turn as the first step to changing your story.

The remarkable change requires patience and dedication. The chrysalis stays enclosed in one position, waiting…until the change is complete, and then a butterfly emerges. Embedded within each of us are diamond-like qualities waiting to be mined, cut and polished. Are you willing to endure the pressure, the cutting and the polishing to bring out the diamond within?

Remember, you are strong! Keep working and making changes.

CHAPTER 7

FRUITION: THE BLOSSOMED FULFILMENT

Be who God meant you to be and you will set the world on fire.

— Catherine of Siena.

Doing homework with my nephew requires hard work, but it is very rewarding. As we sit there for minutes, both working hard, blending and segmenting three-letter words, it is a challenging and fulfilling time for both of us.

My nephew loves a challenge, and he also loves to play. I always make it a necessity for both of us to do a victory dance when we finish his homework. This is because after hard work comes fruition, and that attainment should be enjoyable.

The pain of hard work, discipline and change is short-lived, but the splendour and glory of fruition leaves a lasting imprint in our minds. It is rewarding seeing our dreams and ideas come to life. When the pain of the hard work is gone, it is the product of our dreams that remains.

Regardless of whether what we are working towards is fulfilling a vision for our life or ministry or developing a talent, learning a new skill or improving our character, there is always a desired end goal. That goal is subjective, but we are pleased when our efforts lead to success.

There is a gladdening in the heart, a pure delight when goals are achieved or dreams are actualised. In addition, there is a desire to enjoy the achievement. This is what the blossomed fulfilment stage is about.

As a vivid, graceful butterfly flies by, it is difficult for it to be concealed, even if the insect wants to be hidden. A flower in full blossom is difficult to mask, and *a city on a hill cannot be hidden*. The sparkle and beauty in the fruition stage has its own condition, function and purpose.

In December 2013, I was hanging out at my friend's flat in London when another friend of mine said, "Lupita is so beautiful."

Another friend replied, "Who is Lupita?"

My friend was surprised. "You do not know Lupita? She is the beautiful woman in *Twelve Years a Slave*."

The movie had not come out then, but everyone was keen on seeing it. I did not know Lupita Nyong'o at the time but I was quite interested in seeing who sparked so much interest at my friend's flat. I never imagined that by 2014, barely a year after that conversation in my friend's flat, Lupita would grace many TV screens, covers of magazines, several red carpets and become a household name.

It was almost unheard of not to have heard of Lupita Nyong'o in 2014. This is because she discovered her talent, improved her skills, followed her passion and chased her dreams. Lupita's dream came to fruition, was in full bloom and was obvious to all.

Lupita won an Oscar for best supporting actress and gave a beautiful acceptance speech that brought tears to my eyes. She passionately ended with, "No matter where you are from, your dreams are valid!" Lupita's dream was valid and came to life.

Looking at her earlier years before her stardom, one can see that she evolved through a process and was performing excellently at previous stages as she was working towards her dream.

Lupita Nyong'o, who has Kenyan parents and was born in Mexico, grew up primarily in Kenya and discovered her love for acting at a young age. Studying at Hampshire College in Amherst, Massachusetts, she earned her degree in film in 2003. Upon her return to Kenya during school summer vacation, she discovered that filming for the drama *The Constant Gardener* was happening in her area. Lupita had a deep passion, and she went for the opportunity to learn and grow, joining the set as a production assistant.

Lupita had discovered her love for acting and was inspired along the way by different stars. Also, as she was working as a production assistant, she was further inspired to go for her dream.

Lupita honed her craft as a filmmaker by directing, editing and producing a documentary called *In My Genes*, which followed the stories of several Kenyans who are living with albinism. During these times, Lupita was growing, learning and building capacity. She then became a star of Kenyan television in the TV series *Shuga*.

Her interest in acting kept blossoming, and she wanted to further pursue her interest, so she returned to America to get a master's degree from the Yale School of Drama.[31] At Yale, she won the Herschel Williams Prize for "acting students with outstanding ability" during the 2011–2012 academic year, and she graduated.[32] Even when Lupita had not reached her fruition stage, she was excelling at previous stages and improving herself.

In her previous seasons, Lupita was shining. Her performance on *Shuga* was brilliant, and at Yale School of Drama, she was performing well and won an award for outstanding ability. This was before the international stardom, but she was passionate and working hard.

Her first job out of Yale School of Drama was her breakthrough role in 2013 on *12 Years a Slave* as Patsey. This role put her on a worldwide status; she won the 2014 Academy Award for best supporting actress and received an array of accolades. Lupita Nyong'o is the first Kenyan actress and the first Mexi-

31
"Lupita Nyong'o," Biography.com, accessed March 9, 2016, http://www.biography.com/people/lupita-nyongo-21465383.
32   "School of Drama 2012–2013," Yale University, PDF, accessed February 17, 2014, Bulletin of Yale University Series 108 no. 13, August 30, 2012. http://bulletin.printer.yale.edu/archivepdffiles/Drama/Drama_2012-2013.pdf

can actress to win an Academy Award.[33]

Not only is she a successful actress, but Lupita has become a fashion icon, with red-carpet appearances and pictures in many publications. She has had the rare privilege of gracing the cover of *Vogue* twice in a short time.

Hard work should lead to fruition. How can we enjoy fruition?

The key is to be you. Though a butterfly is destined to fly, it would be a terrible swimmer. In fact, it cannot swim! Everyone has something he or she is great at, an area of ability. We can all shine at something, and the key is to identify what yours is.

The butterfly should not be flying, looking at the fish and thinking, *I wish I could swim like that*; and the fish should not be staring at the monkeys, thinking, *They seem to be having fun; I wish I could climb trees like that.*

They all have different areas to shine. It can be difficult to focus on our own lane, but it is key to bring fruition to the purpose we have been uniquely designed for. If not, you could spend your life trying to bring to fruition someone else's dream, and it would be a futile experience. The key is to be you—the best you!

While learning about Sir Isaac Newton in primary school, I found it funny how a falling apple prompted him to think about gravity while he was sitting under an apple tree. I thought he discovered gravity by chance that anyone could have been sit-

33   Dana Hughes, "Oscar Winner Lupita Nyong'o Is 'the Pride of Africa,'" ABC News, March 3, 2014, http://abcnews.go.com/blogs/entertainment/2014/03/oscar-winner-lupita-nyongo-is-the-pride-of-africa/.

ting under an apple tree and observed a falling apple. As the years went by, I learnt that in addition to being at the right place at the right time, Sir Newton was a phenomenal genius.

He went against the odds of his background and was determined to make a difference. He was born a tiny, premature baby with few chances for survival, and his father died before he was born. His mother remarried an affluent minister when he was three years old, and he lived with his maternal grandmother.[34]

His start in life had an indelible impact on him. Sir Newton showed signs of severe insecurity, and he was known for irrational conduct when defending his merits. He did not have the ideal start in life, and he even threatened to burn down his stepfather's house, but some of his previous life experiences built some kind of capacity in him and helped set him up for his next stage.

He started seeking comfort in books and discovered his love for mechanics and technology.[35] He ended up becoming a mathematician and physicist who is well regarded as one of the most influential theorist in science history. He came up with many theories, including the Three Laws of Motion, which I particularly enjoyed in physics class. With his immense contributions, it is difficult to speak about physics history without talking about Sir Isaac Newton.

With all the great things Sir Newton contributed to society, it is ironic to think that he would have lived his life as a failed

34   "Isaac Newton," Famous Scientists, accessed March 7, 2016, http://www.famousscientists.org/isaac-newton/.
35   "Isaac Newton: The Man Who Discovered Gravity," BBC, accessed March 7, 2016, http://www.bbc.co.uk/timelines/zwwgcdm.

farmer if he did not identify what he was designed for. He may not have been known as the genius, which would have been a loss to society.

His late father was a farmer and he was the only son, and so when he was seventeen, his mother stopped his schooling so he could become a farmer with hopes that he would run the farm successfully. He failed miserably. He did not love farming and did not have the natural flair for it.

It is important to have the right people around who can identify your strengths and nudge you in the right direction. His uncle persuaded his mother to let him go to the University of Cambridge; perhaps he sensed his intellectual abilities and where he could make the most impact.

Sir Newton went against the odds and made a huge impact doing what he loved. It is frightening to think that he may have spent his whole life being miserable at his lack of success as a farmer. After all, his father was a flourishing farmer, and it was his mother's dream for him to succeed at it. He may have beaten himself up and died an unsuccessful farmer, but he discovered what he was designed for, and he went on to make a difference.

Monarch butterflies have black, orange and white wings while Glasswinged butterflies have transparent wings with opaque borders, which are usually dark brown. The monarch butterfly may think, *Why do I not have rare and spectacular wings like the glasswinged butterfly?* and the glasswinged butterfly may think, *Why am I not as vibrant as the monarch butterfly with its colourful wings?*

Both butterflies are the way they are for a reason. The colour and nature of their appearance is for their own survival. The monarch butterfly sequesters poison in its body, so if a predator eats one monarch butterfly, it becomes sick and develops an aversion to any other butterfly that resembles the one that made it ill. Monarch butterflies have colourful wings to reinforce the association between appearance and illness. Meanwhile the glasswinged butterfly, with its almost transparent wings, blends in with the environment and hides itself from predators. In like manner, as difficult as it might be, we should try to not covet other people's gifts. We have all been designed in a certain way that fits our own purpose.

> **Work out/Engage**
>
> *Have you embraced your uniqueness? Do you know what your uniqueness is shaping you for? How can you develop and utilise your uniqueness?*

One person might be able to handle the benefits and challenges of being a famous singer; another person might not have been graced with that ability but might have been graced with the gift of enterprise or even graced with the gift of singing but not fame. Know yourself and discover what you are meant to bring to fruition!

Rest is vital. At the appointed time, the chrysalis opens and emerges a gorgeous butterfly; however, it is not time for take-off. It takes some time before it can fly because its wings are tiny, soft, wet, wrinkly and folded against its body.

The butterfly is usually very tired after it emerges from the chrysalis, and so the butterfly rests. That is very interesting and wise. We all need to learn to rest. After all the energy we put into working brings the fruition we desire, it helps to take a break.

Once the necessary changes have been made, and the desired skills have been learnt, the first step may not be to dive straight in. After progressing to the advanced swimming class and passed off as a great swimmer, the first step should not be to jump into an ocean.

Rest is good, and we are designed to rest to operate at an optimal level.

From studies, scientists discovered sleep is vital in aiding metabolism, immune function, memory, learning and other important functions. Animal and human studies propose that the quantity and quality of sleep have a profound impact on learning and memory. A proper night's sleep improves learning and enhances problem-solving and analytical skills. It enhances our ability to learn mathematics or physics; however, the learning is not restricted to academic learning only. It also aids learning how to play an instrument like the violin, how to drive a car or learn to swim or even how to play tennis or perfect our golf swing. Sleep has many benefits, and in addition to aiding learning, it helps increase concentration levels, improve decision making and enhance creativity.[36]

A resource from the Division of Sleep Medicine at Harvard Medical School suggests that sleep helps learning and memory in two distinct ways. Firstly, a person who is not well

---

36   "Why Sleep is Important," National Heart, Lung and Blood Institute, accessed January 5, 2016, http://www.nhlbi.nih.gov/health/health-topics/topics/sdd/why.

rested cannot focus attention optimally and learn efficiently. It also affects our mood and contributes to making us demotivated and impairs our judgement.

Proper sleep in terms of quality and quantity helps us function adequately throughout the day. Sleep-deprived people are less productive as they take longer to complete tasks, have a slower reaction time, and make more mistakes.[37]

Secondly, sleep has a part to play in the consolidation of memory that is crucial for learning new information.[38] Learning and memory are usually described in terms of three functions (acquisition, consolidation and recall), which are all necessary for proper memory function. Acquisition is the process of introducing fresh information into the brain. The information is unstable and must be strengthened and moved to long-term storage.

Consolidation is the processes by which a memory becomes stable and Recall is the ability to consciously or unconsciously retrieve and access the information after storage. Research suggests that memory consolidation takes place during sleep through the strengthening of the neural connections that form our memories.[39]

Studies show sleep has a vital part to play in memory before and after learning a new task. This shows that both before and after embarking on a new learning undertaking, we should rest. Before a development activity, rest gives us a fresh mind to learn, but also after we have worked, developed and

37   Ibid.
38   "Benefits of Sleep. Healthy Sleep," Division of Sleep Medicine at Harvard Medical School, accessed January 5, 2016, http://healthysleep.med.harvard.edu/healthy/matters/benefits-of-sleep.
39   Ibid.

accomplished, rest refreshes us. From different research, overall agreement proposes that consolidated sleep at night is optimal for learning and memory.[40]

As the caterpillar eats (learns) and grows (builds capacity), it rests to digest its food (rest to absorb knowledge). The chrysalis is also in a position of rest as the changes are occurring on the inside. Rest is very important in process.

After the butterfly rests, it waits for its wings to dry, and a substance called haemolymph is pumped into the wings to make them grow big and strong. After resting, it helps to refresh and reenergise.

There is a need to build ourselves with the right dose of what energises us, to take on the task of making impact. People get energised in various ways—hanging out with certain people who motivate them or doing relaxing activities like exercising or going on retreats.

> **Work out/Engage**
>
> *What energises you? Add proper rest to your daily schedule.*

Rest, reenergise and create ripples.

A higher chance to succeed. From Lupita's story, we see that previous stages can help set us up the future.

Female butterflies lay eggs in a safe place and on the suitable plant for the caterpillar to feed on when it hatches. The layer on the egg serves as food for the newly hatched hungry caterpillar.

The caterpillar eats and grows as much as possible, so the

---

40   Deep P. Sarode, et al., "A Sleep to Remember: The Effects of Sleep on Memory." Journal of the Royal Medical Society 21, no.1. pp. 23 – 34.

transformation in the chrysalis goes smoothly. In the chrysalis, many of the caterpillar cells serve as energy for the growing butterfly cells. Finally, the striking butterfly emerges from the chrysalis. Every step and part of the process prepares us for the next stage in the development towards fruition.

After the butterfly has rested and has pumped up its wings (energise), it is time to fly. It takes a short time before the butterfly masters the art of flying.

Being a skilled swimmer in a swimming pool does not mean we will be able to handle the waters far out in an ocean instantly. If we have never swum in an ocean, we would have to learn and understand the waves and tides and then practise and build our confidence in an ocean.

If we dream and have the right dream or vision for our life, we fulfil the purpose at the great conception stage (realisation, conception, preparation and dedication) and we have the right tools (the ideal mind-set and the wider value), our dreams become strong enough to hatch, moving from that stage to the next.

Subsequently, fulfil the purpose of the "eat and growth" phase (increase in knowledge and build capacity) with the right tools (*id*eal source of knowledge and right people for direction). If we eat and grow enough, we can pupate (make changes and work).

Work out/Engage

Do you know your current stage in your process is building you for something. Are you letting the process shape you?

The remarkable change is where the right mind-set, suitable knowledge, appropriate capacity and direction are put to work. If we achieve the purpose at this stage (make desired changes or work hard to fulfil dreams), and we have the right tools (motivation, support and accountability), there is a higher chance of reaching fruition.

At fruition, the butterfly still needs to master flying before it can fly easily; however, it learns fly. This is because the butterfly learnt and fulfilled every purpose it was meant to at every previous stage. So it is fully equipped to succeed at what it was designed to do (fly and mate).

We will still need to work hard but because we have done what we need to in previous stages, we learn faster. We have a much higher chance to succeed.

butterfly

Be a survivor and sparkle. The beautiful markings, colours and design of its wings are all part of nature's design to aid the butterfly's survival. When flying, they show the vivid colours of their upper wing surfaces, and when they land, they mimic and blend into their natural surroundings to avoid being preyed on.

The wings of the insect have uneven edges to resemble the

borders of a leaf or other items in nature for survival.

Nothing about our form is by chance or by accident.

If a butterfly is so uniquely designed for survival and to fulfil purpose, how much more are you? Shine every step of the way as you work on being all you can be.

The butterfly is a real survivor. Swallowtail butterflies have tails to trick birds. If the bird takes a bite of the tail, the butterfly may be ruffled, but it will be able to live.

The swallowtail that has been bitten by the bird may feel beaten up by life, but it can still fly and pollinate! You are strong. You can push through challenges. Life may ruffle us up, but we can still achieve purpose.

The cycle should never stop. The key purpose of a butterfly in the stage of fruition is to mate, reproduce and lay eggs and be mobile (fly).

> **Work out/Engage**
>
> *How are you going to ensure that the cycle never stops*

The butterfly finds a mate for reproduction and lays eggs. One life cycle is complete, and another is ready to start all over again as female butterflies lay many eggs in their lifetime.

As we actualise fruition, we should aim to start process in a different area of our life. We are meant to keep dreaming and preparing, keep learning and building capacity, keep working towards our goals and making changes and keep making impact. The cycle should not stop!

Bottom Line of the Blossomed Fulfilment

Be you. No one will do a better job at this than you. What I admire about Lupita is her ability to be herself and shine in her own special way. Lupita is known for her beautiful nature both inside and out. People who work with her say her natural beauty and joie de vivre is a breath of fresh air.

We have been knit and formed in a special way for a reason. It was intentional. No one else can get full marks at being you but you. So why not be yourself and tend your own garden? Another person's grass may be green because they have tended it; they have worked hard and improved and enhanced themselves. They are doing the best with what they have.

Work on being your best self, which will not be perfect but will be a solid authentic version! A wise person once said, "When people put in the hard work and make the investments, like everything in life they reap the benefits."

We do not deserve to sparkle because we are the most intelligent, beautiful, articulate, attractive, gifted or wisest. We deserve to sparkle because no one on earth is exactly like us. You should all have confidence in this fact whether you believe it or not. You are not here by chance.

Excel at every stage. After Lupita got her part in *12 Years a Slave*, she still needed to work very hard on the set of the movie, practising and making sure she was performing excellently; however, her deep passion and dedication to her dream and her previous experience of directing, editing, producing and acting in previous stages in her life put her at a higher chance for success.

When we are faithful with little, we learn to be faithful with more. We do not have to have a worldwide platform to start discovering who we are or what we were called to do.

Even though there is a desired end goal, we do not have to be at this stage before we feel like we are sparkling. We can blossom and shine. There is a purpose for the previous stages prior to this.

Lupita was sparkling long before 2014 at different stages of her life, and now in the fruition stage of her career, she is still sparkling. There is beauty in progression. If you are on the right path, keep pushing through; or if perhaps you have not started your journey, you can take the first step. You might even be on wrong path; however, a great story can come out of redirection.

Know you have been gifted to sparkle. There will be challenges along the way, and it is not unheard of to have periods of doubt. Lupita grew up thinking she was not beautiful and that people who looked like her did not appear on her TV screen; however, she did not let that limit her. Her dream was bigger than her limitation. Our dreams and dedication to our purpose should be bigger than our limitations.

Lupita Nyong'o once said that her mother used to tell her, "You can't eat beauty; it doesn't feed you." She did not understand it until finally she realised that *beauty was not a thing that she could acquire or consume, it was something that she just had to be*. She also realised that what her mother meant by "You cannot eat beauty" was, "You cannot rely on how you look to sustain you. What actually sustains us, what is fundamentally beautiful is compassion for yourself and for those around you."[41]

[41] "Lupita Nyong'o: Black Women in Hollywood Honorees Speeches," YouTube video, March 3,

Lupita hopes, "You will feel the validation of your external beauty but also get to the deeper business of being beauty inside."

We have been gifted so beautifully and wonderfully to bring joy and value to those around us with our gifts. That truly makes us sparkle!

The blossomed fulfilment is the glory of the process. The key to sparkling is appreciating process, discovering who we are—our *gifts, talents* and *purpose*. Importantly, it is developing ourselves, building character deep within us and making impact that lasts! Inside every one of us is a flower waiting to bloom, a diamond waiting to be polished and displayed, a gift waiting to be opened, a butterfly waiting to emerge. Do you believe that you have been gifted for something that is eagerly waiting to be actualised?

Remember you are valuable! Keep blooming.

2014, ESSENCE, accessed January 21, 2016, https://www.youtube.com/watch?v=mrD7HGjghrE.

CHAPTER 8

IMPACT: THE RIPPLE EFFECT

The ripple effect of life is that we have been uniquely designed to make impact on people which multiples when they in turn impact others, like a little pebble hitting an ocean.

—Vome Aghoghovbia

What is your legacy? Is the world a better place because you exist? What do you want to be remembered for? Are you making a difference in the lives of people around you? Do you leave people better than you meet them?

There are certain people we cross paths with who leave an indelible imprint; they have immense substance and add such incredible value that we cannot forget the difference they made in our lives. They may be miles away, uncontactable or have even passed away, but the impact they had in our lives is still a strong memory, and the effects of the impact are still in motion.

The main reason we need to undergo process and develop ourselves is so that we can make an impact. Life is about making a difference in people's lives, using our unique design to leave a footprint on the sands of time by touching hearts and lives and doing things that matter.

As time passes, beauty fades, money is spent and jobs change, it is the difference we have made in the life of others and the impact in the world that remains in the hearts of people.

For me, the picture is clearer. I am specially designed and marvellously created to make a difference and be a positive influence on others, to contribute immensely to their lives, help them find the riches within them and give my time, skills, gifts, and riches to make the world a better place.

How am I going to do this? By understanding my uniqueness, finding out what I am designed to do and developing myself to do just that. Where am I going to start? By stretching myself and resolving in my heart that I can do it. How am I going to start making impact? By starting from the person next to me, doing the little I can and doing the best with the resources at my disposal.

We shine, and it brings gladness and honour when we find our purpose and bring our dreams to life. It makes us feel good; we *should* feel good and enjoy the benefits and perks of a job well done, but that is not the ultimate purpose of what we have achieved. The main purpose is to make an impact that goes beyond us.

After the conception, growth and transformation the insect has undergone, the key purpose of the butterfly is not only to be attractive and reproduce. In addition to that, a butterfly helps aid the fulfilment of a purpose that goes beyond itself: it pollinates.

When a tree has been prepared and nourished in the soil, has undergone growth and harsh weather conditions and bears fruit, it does not consume the fruit by itself. The fruit is there to be consumed by others. We should use our experiences and what we have gained to fulfil a purpose—for a greater good.

We make a big difference in the world starting from the person next to us. Every difference made in a single person's life goes a long way.

When we talk about the evolution of technology, certain names will always crop up. Bill Gates, the technologist, business leader and computer programmer, is a classic example.

Bill Gates grew up in Seattle, Washington, with a wonderful and supportive family. He was a voracious reader as a child who dropped out of Harvard University to start Microsoft with his childhood friend Paul Allen. Through technological innovation and keen business strategy, he built the world's largest software business.

Microsoft became the world's largest PC software company, and as a result, Bill Gates became one of the most influential and richest men in the world. He has been stated as the world's wealthiest person many times, from 1995 to 2007, again in 2009, and he is currently the richest person in the world from 2014 through 2016.

When Bill and Paul Allen started Microsoft, their vision of "a computer on every desktop and in every home" seemed implausible to most people. Today, that vision is a reality in many parts of the world, and personal technology is an integral part of society. Bill Gates made a huge impact in technology and made a massive difference in the world as a whole.

What is even more impressive about Bill Gates is that in addition to his outstanding achievements in the technology world, he understands that real sparkle is in making a difference that goes beyond yourself. He is one of the world's leading philanthropists.

In recent years, he retired from working full time at Microsoft and is now concentrating on working with his charitable foundation the Bill and Melinda Gates Foundation.

He says that his philanthropic work has a lot in common with his work at Microsoft. In both cases, he gets to bring together smart people and collaborate with them to solve big, tough problems.

The Bill and Melinda Gates Foundation is steered by the belief that every life has equal value, and the foundation works to help people to lead healthy, productive lives. What a wonderful cause!

The primary aims of the foundation are, globally, to enhance healthcare and reduce extreme poverty, and, in the United States, to expand educational opportunities and access to information technology. The foundation works with partner organisations worldwide to tackle critical problems in four program areas:

» The Global Development Division works to help the world's poorest people lift themselves out of hunger and poverty. It aims to identify and fund high-impact solutions that can help hundreds of millions of people come out of poverty and build better lives.

» The Global Health Division aims to harness advances in science and technology to save lives in developing countries. It involves working to deliver proven tools—including vaccines, drugs and diagnostics—as well as discover ground-breaking new solutions that are affordable and reliable.

» The United States Division works to improve United States high school and postsecondary education and support vulnerable children and families in Washington State. In the United States, the primary focus is on ensuring that all students graduate from high school prepared for college, and that they have an opportunity to earn a postsecondary degree with labour-market value.

» The Global Policy and Advocacy Division seeks to build strategic relationships and promote policies that will help advance their work. It is dedicated to advocacy, policy analysis, and government relations, as well as strengthening philanthropic partnerships and the charitable sector in the United States and other countries.[42]

In addition to The Bill and Melinda Gates Foundation, in 2010, Bill Gates and Warren Buffet started the Giving Pledge, a campaign that encourages the wealthiest people in the world to give a majority of their wealth to philanthropic causes. It now has well over one hundred signatories.

Bill Gates is touching lives with his gifts and having a ripple effect in the world. How can you create ripples?

Impact is stronger with substance. Substance is built based on how well we have developed ourselves, learnt, grown and transformed and how well we have let the process shape and refine us. Substance can be likened to a diamond. A diamond's value, rarity and beauty are judged according to four C's: carat, colour, cut and clarity.

Carat is the weight by which a diamond is measured. By itself, weight does not determine the value of the diamond. Cut, clarity and colour have a huge part to play in the value and rarity. The colour of the diamond has an impact on the value. Colourless diamonds, which can refer to transparency and honesty, are the most desirable since they allow the most refraction of light (sparkle).

Cut is the characteristic that ignites a diamond's fire, sparkle and brilliance. It refers to how well a diamond was cut. It is one of the most important factors in judging a diamond's quality. A quality-cut diamond will be more brilliant and reflect light more strikingly.

---

42   What we do, Bill and Melinda Gates Foundation, accessed March 18, 2016, http://www.gates-foundation.org/

The brilliance of a diamond depends heavily on its cut. The more we go through process and allow ourselves be shaped and transformed, and the more we work hard to improve our skills, develop character and become better, the more our inner value will shine. The function of the cut is to display the diamond's intrinsic beauty to the greatest extent possible and this is what process and growth helps us do—brings out the beauty that was deep inside us all along.

A diamond's clarity is the absence of inclusions in the diamond. It is the measure of inclusions that can be seen, which are the internal or external flaws in the diamond. Nearly all diamonds, even those of the highest quality, have some inclusions.

Clear diamonds create more brilliance and thus are more valued; however, it is rare to have perfect clarity and no flaws. The relative visibility of the inclusions in the diamond and their impact on the overall visual appearance is checked to grade the precious gemstone. We will not be free of flaws and imperfections, but the overall impact they have on us and how they affect us should be looked at. The more we know how to manage our flaws and imperfections, the more we sparkle.

The size, number and severity of these inclusions determine the clarity and the grade of a diamond. As we remove negative traits and build positive habits by developing ourselves, building our character and learning positive disciplines, we have

Work out/Engage

What one thing are you going to do to improve yourself? (More substance)

more substance.

No one is perfect. Nearly all diamonds contain tiny natural birthmarks that are present to varying degrees. After all, nature is seldom perfect, and neither are diamonds; however, these marks serve as the identifying "fingerprint" that makes every gemstone unique.

We are so unique that even our imperfections make us unique individuals, and we are still valuable despite them. It is the ability to manage them that polishes the diamond within us and makes us sparkle even more.

Impact has a momentum. Physics can be used to explain the effects of impact and what happens when two objects (people) collide (interact) with each other. Every moving object has momentum, a product of the mass of the object and its velocity.

Momentum (vector) = Mass (magnitude) Velocity (direction)

The effect of the impact individuals make can be broken down into two parts. First, mass (amount of matter in an object) refers to the substance in the individual.

Next, velocity (speed of an object in a given direction) refers to the zeal in us. This is the enthusiastic devotion to a cause and the enthusiasm with which a person wants to use the substance within them to make impact in a particular direction.

Impact *(momentum)* = ***Substance*** *(mass)* ***Zeal*** *(velocity)*

When we interact with people, the effectiveness of our impact will depend on the substance in us and the zeal to make a difference with that substance. It is difficult to change the direction of an object that is moving with a lot of momentum.

The strength of impact can be explained if, for example, we look at toy cars and collisions. Children are playing with toy cars, and two cars are moving towards each other; suddenly there is a loud bang. The collision leads to more than a sound. When the cars collide, momentum (impact) is transferred form one car to the other.

Assuming elastic collision (type of collision), as a red car in motion runs into an immobile black car of equal mass, the red car stops moving while the black car is set in motion.

If two individuals have the same substance within them, but one person has zeal to make a difference while the other does not, the individual with determination will be more impactful.

When a big red car collides with a small black car at the same speed, they both have impact on each other, but the big red car will have greater effect on the small black car. The more substance in us, the more useful or fruitful impact we can make on others.

That said, when two cars with equal mass and speed collide, the two cars bounce off each other, exchanging equal momentum. People with similar substance and zeal will make similar levels of impact on each other. They will both exchange ideas

Work out/Engage

What type of impact are you making? How deep is your substance and how zealous are you to make impact with that substance? How effective is your impact?

and bounce value off each other.

There are even some more indelible interactions like inelastic collision. In perfectly inelastic collision, when two objects collide, they stick together and move with the same speed in the same direction, regardless of their mass or velocity before the collision.

This kind of influence leads to two people having combined substance and the same level of zeal after they interact. They move together in the same direction, regardless of their initial direction.

These examples show the strength of interactions. We all make an impact on the people we interact with. "As iron sharpens iron, so one person sharpens another."[43]

Impact creates ripples. A small pebble that is dropped into an ocean hits the ocean, and even though the impact is made in a small spot in that vast ocean, the impact creates a ripple effect.

The impact of the little pebble thrown into a pond causes an indirect effect that spreads out from the main effect to reach areas far removed from its original target.

Impact made on even a single person multiples as that person further impacts other people. We sometimes think the impact we make is small or our light lacks lustre, but it usually goes further than we think.

Every word, action and deed has an effect that can create ripples.

We all make ripples. What type of ripples do we make?

[43] Proverbs 27:17 (NIV).

How far do they travel? How do they influence others?

The distance the ripples travel is the influence of the pebble. We should aim to have a strong enough impact that it travels far enough to make huge influence.

My math tutor was doing his job, but he did his job excellently. He was doing his duty, and if he thought he was making little impact on just a single little nine-year-old girl with ponytails, he was mistaken.

It was not until years later that I fully got to understand the ripple effect. I started understanding the value of influence when I started tutoring secondary school students in mathematics and science during my time at university.

The tutoring started when a parent asked my sister if I could help tutor their son for his entrance exams. I was really excited, as any opportunity to do mathematics is a great opportunity to me. I was eighteen or nineteen years old at the time, and I was really looking forward to my first teaching session.

I tutored him for two days and loved tutoring. One thing I always remembered and that stuck with me from my two-day session with him was the excitement on his face when I taught him an easier way to learn and understand Pythagoras's Theorem.

There was a genuine excitement on the boy's face, like he had found gold. When I was nine years old, I was playing around with a pen and paper, and I learnt an easy and short way to learn the theorem. I found it so amazing how something that was fun to me was impacting someone else deeply.

I started tutoring others after that. It makes me glad when they make remarks like "Mathematics is not that bad after all" or "It seems so easy now." It particularly gives me immense joy when I see them do exceptionally well. The joy with which they excitedly rush to tell me their exceptional results or the great things they are doing always brings a smile to my face, which shows I am so proud of them each time. A lot of them have gone on to get exceptional results and do great things.

Each time, I feel their success is my joy, whether it is the students I only tutored twice or the ones I tutored for months. What was the point of getting full marks in mathematics if I could not use it to somehow impact others? Yes, getting those grades made me happy and brought some kind of butterfly moment to my life, but that should not be all there is to it. Anything that

> **Work out / Engage**
>
> *Is there a gift or talent you have that you are not using for the benefit of others? Think of one way you can start using it to benefit others and start!*

makes me shine should be used for the good of others.

And this is how my amazing tutor whom I have not seen in many years, completely unaware of the impact he has made, went on to create a ripple effect that has spread onto many other young people. This is because he taught in an impactful way. Do not ever think your mission is too small. Excellence at whatever you do makes more of an impact than you think.

Not everyone will have the patience for tutoring, but you can help people in several ways. It could be through encouragement, using your resources to support others, helping others develop, or using your skills to meet a need. Use your achievement and experiences to meet a need beyond you!

Pollinating Butterfly

Impact is like a butterfly that pollinates. The butterfly can keep flying around, looking gorgeous. After all, it has gone through all the processes to become this creature, but in addition to being pleasing to watch, it goes around fulfilling a greater purpose. It pollinates flowers (makes an impact).

Pollination is essential to the survival of plants because it is part of their reproductive process. It is equally important for human beings, because without pollination, we would not have vegetables and fruits to eat. Nature designs the flower and the butterfly in such a way that as the butterfly takes nectar from different flowers, it picks up pollens and contributes to pollination. As a butterfly nourishes itself, it also becomes one of nature's migratory pollinators and makes a difference to plants and even human beings.

Finding something that gives you joy, is in line with your unique design, and impacts people at the same time is bliss.

True leadership is about impact and influence—the value you are adding and how far it travels in ripples.

As a true leader grows, that growth impacts the people who follow; and in the leader's absence, the impact should last. Leadership is not teaching people to solely depend on you; it is helping people discover the diamond within them, mining, cutting, and polishing it so they can stand on their own and start positively influencing others even in your absence.

A true leader is identified when, after he or she has left a place, he or she is deeply missed, but the place can stand and survive as a result of the impact the leader has made and the systems he or she has put in place.

True shining comes from being able to make a big difference in a person's life. We can make an impact that lasts and create widespread influence by helping others discover lasting riches.

We should not only be seeking to find our own riches or only aiming to use those gifts to help others, we should also be helping others find their own riches and gifts. Also we should be helping others realise that they deserve to sparkle.

Work out/Engage

Think of someone you can help develop. In what ways can you help this person? Make out time and help to develop the person.

As Benjamin Disraeli said, "The greatest good you can do for another is not just to share your riches but to reveal to him his own."

Bottom Line of the Ripple Effect

Make a difference that sets the world on fire. All the exceptional people I have written about in this book made an impact in their own special way by chasing their dreams.

Rowland Hussey Macy chased his passion, navigated seasons, and evolved through his process. The unique marketing strategies that he innovatively established set precedence for the retail industry as we know it today.

Debbie Sterling, through her experiences of her misconceptions of engineering and her challenges of being an engineering student, birthed her dream. She is helping girls build confidence in problem-solving and improving their spatial skills while they have fun. Her dream was fuelled by her desire to inspire the next generation of female innovators and engineers by creating a toy that will spark their interest in engineering. She is using her passion to make a ripple effect in the lives of young girls.

Nola Ochs and Colonel Sanders show that you can make great impact regardless of age or background. Nola Ochs was still inspiring people at the age of one hundred as she was in the process of writing a book. She has inspired people to keep learning and growing and to realise that it is never too late to go for your dreams. Colonel Sanders inspired others by achieving his goal of selling his secret recipe for fried chicken, leaving an example that we can chase after our passion even at the age of sixty-two.

Susan Cain did research and wrote a book to make introverts like me understand ourselves better and the power of our personality. She went through a process and is using her experience to teach people the strength of their personality.

Sheryl Sandberg is inspiring women to lean in and be bold

to reach the top of their careers. She went through the process herself and is using her experience and insight to encourage and inspire other women.

The legacy Alfred Nobel left behind is still honouring great men and women from all around the world for their great accomplishments in physics, chemistry, medicine, literature, and for work toward achieving peace.

Marie Curie, stood out in her time and became the first woman to win a Nobel Prize, the only woman to win twice, and the only person to win in two different sciences, physics and chemistry. She made great contributions to science that are still being used today.

Sir Isaac Newton contributed immensely to physics and came up with many theories like the Universal Law of Gravitation and Newton's Three Laws of Motion (which I enjoyed in physics class!), and he ended up impacting the world.

Lupita Nyong'o chased her passion and fulfilled her dreams. Her presence on TV screens and magazines is inspiring other girls and women like her to know that their dreams are valid and they are beautiful. Lupita is making waves of impact, giving talks and letting young girls know that she hopes that "they will feel the validation of their external beauty but also get to the deeper business of being beauty inside."

What is your unique mission?

Be generous with your life. The questions to ask ourselves are: What can I do to make a difference? What have I been uniquely created to do? What is my mission and purpose?

Then take action to develop the answers and aim to make that difference, no matter the magnitude. We all have something deposited in us that the world needs. Suppressing what we have been created to offer is of no use or value to anyone.

Let's get to the deeper business of mining that diamond rough, going into the chrysalis, discovering those gifts; and let us use it to bear fruit for the benefit of others.

That special and unique gift that we brought out of the box, that diamond that has been cut and polished, that dollar that we found hidden in our wallet, that tree that has produced sweet fruit should all be used to create a ripple effect.

As Anthony Fauci said, "I believe I have a personal responsibility to make a positive impact on society." As we work towards becoming all we were designed to be, our aim should be to make a lasting impact according to our unique purpose.

Let us learn to be generous with our lives. Let us use our gifts, riches, talents, and time to serve others and contribute to society. Develop a heart that wants to see people better off.

Start today. Navigate *seasons* by knowing what season you are in, and understanding and preparing for the season. Learn from the past, plan for the future, withstand stormy seasons and thrive in blooming times.

Understand *process* is step-by-step. Although the process might include pain, evolve through a process to bring out your unique sparkle to a greater degree.

Birth n*ewness*, embark on something new, prepare inwardly and you might just discover something remarkable.

Experience *growth* by starting the cyclical process of learning and building capacity. Learning is living!

Undergo *transformation* by taking a step in the right direction or if you discover that you are walking in the wrong direction, make a U-turn. Be dedicated to your transformation and surround yourself with supporters, motivators and encouragers.

The best way to enjoy *fruition* is to be you, the best you.

Make *impact* by developing yourself and using your unique design to make a difference that creates ripples.

The purpose of the whole process is to embrace yourself, develop and make lasting impact. You can make impact regardless of age, gender, class, background or circumstances. '*Be an example and set an example in what you say, in the way you live, in your love, in your faith and in integrity*'[44].

The ripple effect is the path to greatness. Believe that you have been specially designed to make meaningful contributions. Every individual matters. Every individual deserves to sparkle. Every individual has a part to play in making a difference. You want to make a difference? Start with the person next to you! Your unique sparkle and brilliance should give light to the world. Be generous with your life!

Remember, you are impactful! Keep making ripples.

Sparkle During the Journey

Ultimately, the moment I understood that I was specifically designed to be a unique individual and to make a difference that creates ripples, I began to love the transformative process of fully becoming that person. I have been:

» The adventurous, creative six-year-old with an active mind

» The Disney-loving girl who loves to write and dance

» The mathematics-loving adolescent who loves to solve complex problems

» The shy, reserved teenager who lives in her own bubble

» The blossoming young adult who started finding herself

» The young woman with interesting and diverse experiences

I discovered that all I have been and all I am, is shaping me for something beyond me. I am not there yet, but I am learning and growing every day.

I do know that not being at your destination does not stop

you from sparkling along the way.

I am fully becoming who I was designed to be.

It is a beautiful, ongoing process.

I am learning to embrace every aspect of my uniqueness.

What I am certain of, though, is I deserve to sparkle…and you do, too.

Everyone deserves to sparkle!

ACKNOWLEDGMENTS

'No man is an island'

– John Donne

Blossoming into the individual who knows she deserves to sparkle, has involved many motivators, encouragers and supporters. There are many people who have impacted my life at different stages. I would like to thank:

My family for being part of creating many of the wonderful memories I write of in this book.

My parents, Mr Godfrey and Mrs Ese Aghoghovbia, who have sacrificed for their daughters. They love us dearly and never failed to give us the best. Growing up in a society where the girl child is sometimes seen as second rate, we grew up confident that we could reach for the stars. I cannot thank my parents enough for all the love, sacrifices and the great legacy that I will pass on to my children.

My sisters, Voke, Vona and Vese who have been my best friends and cheerleaders. Thanks for all the memories. For all the games we played, all the times we danced, laughed and cried together. Thanks for listening to my stories and encouraging me to write. For cheering me on and being a solid support system. Life would simply not have been the same growing up without three of you.

To **my best friend, Tunde Gafaar,** who never fails to tell me how much of a bright star I am. Thank you for believing strongly in me and for being very supportive. Thanks for reading for exams with me, reviewing job applications with me and reading through this book time and time again even on weeks you had on call shifts. Thanks for motivating me to write and encouraging me to be and do my best.

To **my brothers, Yemi, Uche and Kunle**, who have been the best brothers I could have hoped for. Thank you for supporting me and being there for me. For the heavy lifting, for the inspirational talks and for the encouragement.

To **my Nephew and Niece, Tamilore and Tanure**, who bring so much joy to my life.

To **my Pastors, Dr Sola and Pastor Bimbo Fola-Alade**, who have been caring and wonderful pastors. Your care and inspirational messages have impacted my life immensely.

To **aunty Gladys, my wonderful aunty** who stayed up all night listening to my countless stories and discussed 'the solar planets' and 'factors of production' with me. You encouraged me to grow in creativity and confidence.

To **my maths tutor, Mr Ojimmy**, for your patience to bring out the sparkle in me. Your amazing work shaped my life and is helping to shape the life of many.

To the amazing **institutions** that have added so much value to my life, **University College London (UCL)**, **Vivian Fowler Memorial College for Girls** and **Pampers Private School**.

To **my brother, Rabin Ojoh** and **my childhood friends and sisters, Onyeka and Omono**, who explored and went on many adventures with me. Thank you for always taking part in my outlandish ideas.

To the **Teenagers at The Liberty Church** and the **students** I have tutored mathematics and science, I do not take the responsibility lightly. The opportunity to teach you has helped me grow and develop. Thank you for allowing me have an impact in your lives.

To **The Liberty Church**, where I have experienced Church in the most life changing way. By volunteering there, I have learnt about service, sacrifice and leadership. I have the best Church family.

To **Yemi Gafaar and Arike Rabiu**, for reading through the manuscript and giving constructive feedback.

To **3Alphastudios**, for all the hard work, designing the cover page and interior of the book.

To **Bimbo Dare**, my lovely editor. Thanks for the hard work.

To my grandparents, aunts and uncles, teachers, cousins, friends…

… and to the many people who have one way or the other *contributed* to my sparkle, THANK YOU!

Printed in Great
Britain
by Amazon

31926484R00097